Little Slices of My Life

MARICE KATZ

AuthorHouse™
1663 Liberty Drive
Bloomington, IN 47403
www.authorhouse.com
Phone: 1-800-839-8640

© 2010 Marice Katz. All rights reserved.

No part of this book may be reproduced, stored in a retrieval system, or transmitted by any means without the written permission of the author.

First published by AuthorHouse 5/13/2010

ISBN: 978-1-4520-1406-7 (sc)

Library of Congress Control Number: 2010905587

Printed in the United States of America
Bloomington, Indiana

This book is printed on acid-free paper.

The Jewish Georgian

Reporting to the Jewish Community of Georgia

April 6, 2010

To Whom It May Concern:

For many years, we have been honored to have articles written by Ms. Marice Katz published in *The Jewish Georgian*. It is our understanding that Ms. Katz now plans to have these pieces compiled into a book, which is to be published by an entity other than *The Jewish Georgian*.

Since this material has been copyrighted by us, please accept this letter as our authorization for the publication of these articles by other entities of Ms. Katz's selection, provided that attribution is given to *The Jewish Georgian*.

Sincerely

Marvin Z. Botnick
Publisher

MZB/gw

~ 8495 Dunwoody Place, Suite 100 ~ Atlanta, Georgia 30350 ~
- 404-236-8911   Fax 404-236-8913 -

Marice's Chicken Soup   *September–October 2004*

So-o-o-o many people have asked me how I happened to start writing articles for the JEWISH GEORGIAN paper that I decided to address that subject.

First time it came up, Gene Asher owned the paper. He came up to see me at my office one day and asked if I would write an article about how my career in Finance started. I said, "Gosh, I can't do that- I have never written anything – maybe you could just have someone interview me instead". He still insisted that I should write about it. Well, that was that because I still didn't think I could do it.

A good while after that, Marsha LaBeaum, editor of paper, made a luncheon appointment with me and during the entrée she asked if I would write an article, just as Gene had suggested. I said no, continuing to think that I could not do it.

That very night I was sitting in the living room and I found a pen in my hand and paper suddenly in my lap – the pen just started writing (I had nothing to do with it)! And writing! And writing! I was completely lost in my memories of 41 years ago when I came to this wonderful city in 1963 for an interview for a secretarial position at The Robinson-Humphrey Company and my subsequent first day on the job, June 5th. I loved doing it; the article practically wrote itself. I never expected to be in the category of Vida Goldgar (who we will all sorely miss), Cynthia Tucker, or Lewis Grizzard, but I just kept finding little slices of my life I wanted to tell people about – my personal Chicken Soup for the Soul. And I have never had any regrets about writing these articles. I think it is time to thank Gene, Marvin, and Marsha for this privilege – and all the people who have expressed to me the enjoyment they receive reading my articles.

Someday, I may even write a book- they say everyone has a book in them – We will see!

Suddenly – 45 Years   *July–August 2008*

It went fast but along came June 5 and I was being wined and dined in honor of my anniversary with my company. It was very touching and I deeply appreciated all the tributes I received. Somehow they got a copy of the article I had written for the Jewish Georgian newspaper about the beginning of those years. That article was written in 1996 and was the first one I had ever written for the Jewish Georgian. It is reproduced below:

Taking Stock: 30 Years
    With The Robinson-Humphrey Co.   *January-February 1996*

On a Sunday in April 1963 I stood in front of the Rhodes-Haverty building in downtown Atlanta shaking my head. My job interview with The Robinson-Humphrey Company was the next morning and I wanted to stake out where I needed to go so I wouldn't be late for the appointment... I was not prepared for this old building. Surely everything would be gleaming, shiny and new in this metropolis. This was a disappointment to me. But in December 1981 when we moved to a shiny new building in Buckhead, the Sunday when we all went in to arrange our new offices, was one of the saddest I ever spent. I cried the whole day. I had grown to love the Rhodes-Haverty building and downtown Atlanta.

So, you now know that I did get the job at the stock brokerage company. I moved from North Carolina on May 31, and started work on June 5. When I arrived in Atlanta, I found a furnished apartment and stayed there six months. I furnished my next place with every bargain I could find: The gentleman at the furniture store pulled out a repossessed chair for my living room, a kitchen table that had been collecting dust in the basement for years, and a convertible sofa that had been reduced and reduced. I used to describe it as "no, not contemporary – early bargain furniture".

The personnel man and I negotiated my salary so I ended up with $375 a month, but I got a raise after three months. I was in a secretarial pool at first; eventually I was chosen to work with one of the senior producers, Mr. Sidney Smith. It was about this time I started studying to fulfill my long time dream of becoming a stock broker. And did I study!—on the bus to and from work, in the beauty shop, while I ate lunch and dinner, and on weekends. I took the home course offered by the New York Institute of Finance, so I was on my own. The exam was given at Emory University. The day I was told by one of the head men that I had passed, I keeled over from happiness. This man thought I was dead, and was a "little" upset until I started laughing and beaming.

The world was different back then. There was very little technology, and it was not a global market, but many of the problems we dealt with back then exist today. I kept absorbing everything I could about the market and learning all I could from Sidney Smith, as well as Lewis Holland who worked with him at the time. The memories are many. When John F Kennedy was shot, for one, we all stood around in shocked disbelief. There was a date in October 1987 when the stock market reeled, and the Gulf War in 1990.

There was such friendliness and warmth in every single person in Atlanta. My mother died six months before I came to Atlanta, my father died two weeks before I was born, and my oldest brother had died some years ago—so maybe such southern kindness, which seemed to be everywhere, meant more to me than it would to most. I fell in love with it and immediately felt at home.

I was also in love with the market and investing in general, so I did not mind working long hours, staying up past midnight, especially when Sidney Smith died. He was a man of the greatest integrity, and his death was a stunning loss to the investment community. At the time, I teamed up with Harold Goldstein, a brilliant person whom I was lucky to have as a mentor. It was then that I began my career as a financial consultant in earnest. Also, at this point American Express bought the company; we became a division of Shearson, and many changes were taking place. I could not believe how exciting it all was.

I remember my first order, and not believing I was getting paid for something I enjoyed doing so much. I began getting corporate titles, taking and studying every area that would improve my knowledge. When Harold died in 1993, another sadness descended on me.

Again the company was sold, this time to Travelers, and we became a division of Smith Barney. But in 1993, when I was given a 30th anniversary party, the closeness of the Robinson-Humphrey Company was never more evident as everyone helped me celebrate. It has been nearly 33 years since I began my career. In that time, I have gone from not knowing if I had 20 cents for a box of tissues to a dream come true. All those years dedicated to that dream! Any regrets? So Far—no.

Aftermath:
And I still have no regrets in this year of 2008.

All work and no play?
   Try a week away   *November–December 1997*

Long weekends are a nice way to vacation, but after ten years of this it occurred to me that maybe a week away would be desirable. I thought about it quite a while. Would my business fall apart if I were gone that long? Would I get restless being away from my routine for eight days? I had seen a couple of ants in my kitchen and I wondered if an army of them would take over while I was gone.

As you can see, I had plenty of doubts and qualms. However, I called my travel agent and said I had always wanted to see Cape Cod. She immediately recommended a tour, and sent me literature to look over. With great trepidation, I finally made my reservation. Now, you might think it sounds silly to be so skittish about taking a vacation, but it was a big deal for me. I was scheduled to leave in September, and so two weeks in advance I pulled out my suitcase and started packing a little bit each night. I was advised to take as little as possible—but I am a woman. I packed and unpacked the suitcase.

Eventually, I packed every T-shirt I own with Atlanta printed on it. I felt I could make it with those and two pairs of jeans.

With all those bon voyage parties I was given, you would think I was sailing to Europe for several months. It might as well have been for all the planning I did. The fateful day arrived, and it was the most beautiful day I have ever witnessed. I was soon sailing through the air, telling my seat companion all about what I was going to see and do. He got so excited that he picked up the plane phone and tried to call his travel agent to book the same tour – but alas, it was to no avail.

I safely landed in Boston a couple of hours later, and was soon ensconced in the Swissotel, where I met all kinds of fascinating people who were also going on the tour. I was suddenly feeling so perky about everything that I hardly slept a wink that night. Bright and early the next morning, we left for our first destination. Never having been in New England before, I was entranced. Each place we visited was more enchanting than the last. Each inn or hotel was nicer than the last. Each meal was more delicious than the last. Martha's Vineyard was one of my most favorite places, but each spot was delightful. Our final day was spent in Plymouth, Massachusetts. To see the Mayflower and the rock where the pilgrims first stepped in 1620 was like experiencing history itself.

The trip was over much too soon. I was very happy to be home though. My exterminator had done his usual good job before I left and the ants had not taken over. I did not have time to get restless on my vacation. Back at the office, my clients seemed real happy that I had treated myself to time off, and the market behaved itself in my absence. The lovely couple from England who invited me to visit them (and have already written encouraging notes asking me to do so) give me reason to think I won't wait another ten years to take a week's vacation.

Standing at the Crossroads of Life.   *January-February 1998*

The radio comes on at 7:00 a.m. A really nice tune is playing and a new day begins. But I am caught up in memories and lie in bed a little longer than usual. It is December 29. In a couple of days, the old year will end and the astounding fact is that 1998 will be here soon. Major events in my life start parading through my mind. The growing-up years in my hometown of Durham, North Carolina, the summers spent at Virginia Beach, my first marriage proposal when I was 18, graduating from school, going to college and away from home to work.

To quote the Torah, "Life is but a fleeting moment". I am caught up thinking about just that—wondering how all these years could have gone by so swiftly, each one becoming more and more precious. I keep thinking how different things would have been for me if, when I was standing there at the fork in the road, I had turned right instead of left, or gone straight ahead, or not moved at all—just stopped and picked the daisies right there. So much I missed, perhaps.

These are not sad thoughts, because I feel truly blessed with a wonderful life. However, I can't help but wonder how it would have turned out if I had stepped in another direction. I am just sentimental at this momentous time of year. Somehow, unbelievably, a new song is playing on the radio: "….Should auld acquaintance be forgot….." How appropriate to my thoughts. How exciting to know that in another two years, the new millennium will be upon us, and in this enlightened age of technology, new insights will lead the way.

I decide how much better it is to look forward rather than backward. I say my morning prayers and dash for the shower and my future—as the strains of the song "Now is the Hour" follow me.

The Mouse That Roared—Mastering A New Computer Is Not The Katz Meow   March-April 1998

For two years, management had been telling us that we were getting a new computer system. They used words like "wonderful," "magnificent," and "state-of-the-art." Now, I loved my old computer – I was used to it and it was fine – so I dreaded having to get used to something else. But I figured, oh well, it's like going to the dentist – the dread is worse than the actuality. Wrong, wrong, wrong! It turned out to be a nightmare.

We went into the office on a Sunday for two hours of training. That wasn't so bad – but Monday was bad. We were in and out of classes all day. Guys who may have been having a hard time themselves rallied together and made fun of me. I simply told the truth: "I hate it." In return, I got comments like, "well, you can't teach an old dog new tricks," and "you would be happy if you were still under the buttonwood tree" (where the Stock Market started in 1792). I was in tears.

Then, there was the mouse! I hate to admit it, but I never had used one before and it was a struggle. But, one of the computer experts gave me a couple of tips, and so things began to look up. This same person told me not to feel so diminished. He had mastered computers in first grade, and now kindergartners were on top of it.

Well, Tuesday was a lot better. By Wednesday, the last day of classes, I was sailing along. I felt pretty vindicated when one of the big talkers came into my office to ask me how to do something.

A thirty-five year old client told me, "Marice, I'm proud of you. Learning that new stuff will keep you young." She said she wasn't learning anything.

I now know that I can be as friendly with the new computer as I was with the old one. It really is amazing.

Though Thick and Thin *May – June 1998*

First, there was the stationary bicycle. It was really uncomfortable, so I sold it and bought a more expensive one. It seemed a good fit in the store, but after three months, I hated it. Even the seat cushion my sister in California sent couldn't fix it.

Then came the daily walk after I got home from the office. During the fall, I really enjoyed it, but eventually, it got cold and dark early.

I love to swim, so I began making the trip to the AJCC every day. I thought that would work, but I began finding excuses not to make the trek. By then, the athletic club in my office building opened, and I started swimming there every day. But, the water was so cold that after a year of this, I gave up.

I heard of the Health Rider, and rushed to the mall to buy one. By the time the trial period ended, I developed such pains in my arms that I headed to the orthopedist, who advised me to get a treadmill—so I did!

Success! I am at last getting proper exercise, enjoying it, and not finding excuses. When I get into a smaller-size dress, I'll know it was really worthwhile.

This Vacation Was All Wet   *July–August 1998*

Last fall I had a great time in Cape Cod, so I decided that taking a week off now and then was not such a bad idea. So, it was back to the travel agent.

On prominent display at the agency was a glossy brochure featuring the most gorgeous ship. I'd been on cruises before, but it was long ago, and I was finally ripe for another one – sun, sea, blue skies, and some sand. My mouth watered. I mentioned all this to a cousin in New York and she decided to go also.

We set sail from Miami. The ship was not a disappointment and the food was excellent. The entertainment was the best (including me in the Karaoke bar singing "Rhinestone Cowboy" from the bottom of my heart – off key, of course). But I never expected what transpired.

I had dreamed of waves lulling me to sleep, but here was a raging ocean – and at 2:00 a.m. We had returned to our room, my cousin from the casino and I from the Karaoke bar, and we needed some rest. The ship was like the Titanic, rocking and rolling to the beat of the band. This was what the word "turbulent" was invented to describe.

Bleary-eyed at breakfast the next morning, the captain announced that the roughness was a result of the tornadoes in Northern Florida. When you're beaten down, it is uplifting to have an explanation. (Ha!)

It was not just one night of tumult – it was the general rule. There was the morning on deck, where, with a very nice gentleman, I was deep in conversation about life in the North vs. life in the South. We were talking away when – can you believe it – a tremendous wave suddenly washed right over us. Sopping wet, that was me. If someone had described to me such an incident, I would have thought it was a "Titanic"-inspired tall tale. But believe me, it's true.

The stops in Mexico and Key West were fun, but the couple next to me in the dining room was not. They both had colds and constantly sneezed in my direction. A few days after the cruise, when the temperature dropped twenty degrees, I came down with a first-class cold.

Damn the torpedoes! Full speed ahead! But without me next time…

Goldberg's Serves The Staff of Life
  And The Stuff of Laughs   *September-October 1998*

It's not a very big place but it sure packs a wallop. Delightful aromas abound and there are so many choices—nova, wonderful corned beef, made-on-the-premises breads, all sorts of sweet delectables, and my favorite, dill pickles in the barrel. And lest we forget—the bagel. By now, you must know that I'm talking about Goldberg's, home of the Bagel Boys.

Owners Wayne and Howard are from South Africa. Do you ever wonder what it would be like to move to another country? How hard it might be to become part of a different culture? Well, these two ambitious, but gentle and caring, guys have done it by endearing themselves to all who know them.

It's not the old corner drugstore, but in 1998, it's the next best thing. The wonderful food notwithstanding, the great thing about Goldberg's is that you can hear the best jokes in town there.

Here's one:
Two bees meet up one day. Bee #1 asks Bee #2 how he is. Bee #2 replies that he's not doing too well because he hasn't had much to eat lately. Bee #1 says, "Oh, there is a Bar Mitzvah reception down the street this afternoon. There's going to be lots of good stuff there—wine, cake topped with honey, and strawberries and pineapple covered in whipped cream. You need to head down there right now." A couple of hours later, the bees meet again. Bee #1 asks how did you make out, and he says fine, thank you. Then Bee #1 says, "What's that funny black bump on your head"? Bee #2 replies, "It's a yarmulke." "Why in the world are you wearing that?" #1 asks. Bee #2 says, "I didn't want them to think I was a wasp."

A touch of New York (not to mention South Africa) has invaded the South, and Atlanta will never be the same again—and in this case, that's a good thing. If you will excuse me now, I have to finish my lox and cream cheese on an Everything bagel!

That Sinking Feeling — November–December 1998

It was 7:30 on a Saturday night, and I was exhausted because I had been celebrating my birthday all week. However, I was having three out-of-town guests for brunch the next morning, and figured I had better prepare the main dish in order to be ahead of the game.

This main dish was an egg casserole that called for a hundred ingredients, the principal one being twelve eggs. I laid out everything I needed, and painstakingly cracked each egg, throwing the shells into the garbage disposal. Although the disposal was running, the water wouldn't go down the drain. Over and over again, I fooled with it.

Finally, I called my regular plumbing service, but "Joe" said they were short-handed and everyone was out on an emergency. The next service said they would call back in fifteen minutes; I still haven't heard from them. By the time I got the sixth plumber on the line, I was in tears. He said it would cost about $265 for him to come out after hours, but if I could wait till the morning, regular rates would apply. However, he couldn't guarantee that he'd be out there first thing in the a.m.

Then he said, "Listen, lady, have you got a plunger?" I said I did, and he told me to get it. The first time I tried to plunge the sink, I got water all over the counter, floor, and me. The guy patiently talked me through it and after a few more tries – Eureka! It worked!

At this point, I was crying with joy as he told me to let the hot water run for a while. I told him he was a genius. He asked me to call his service manager Monday and tell her that. I gladly agreed to do so. The brunch went as planned, and it was delicious.

While that's the end of the story, it does remind me of another one. A man I know called a plumber, who came out and fixed his problem in fifteen minutes. When he was handed the bill, the man said, "For goodness sake! I didn't make that much money when I was a surgeon!" The plumber replied, "Well, neither did I."

As time Marches On, So Should You   January-February 1999

These days, the world seems to be spinning faster and faster, hurtling through space at a rapid pace. Technology is king. We have left the Age of Aquarius for the Age of the internet. Computer savvy qualifies a 17-year old to start a company instead of seeking a college education. Pundits debate what moniker to pin on the waning decade. Some say that it was unmemorable, almost Dullsville. Far be it for me to argue, although I will shake my head in disbelief.

Is this an exciting time? Yes. Are these days tumultuous? Yes.

Would it be wise to get in the way of progress? No.

Because we all occasionally yearn for the good old days, we often, in turn, wonder where we are headed. As long as we strive to make our own lives better, to help others, and enjoy a truly fine musical arrangement, a magnificent sunrise or sunset, a good book, a warm slice of apple pie with vanilla ice cream, the ability to laugh and still find humor in even the most mundane things, and sustain our belief in America and in the basic goodness of most people, then I think we can accept that change is inevitable and go along for the ride.

The Method May Have Changed, But Love Still Springs Eternal *March–April 1999*

How times do change! When my mother was sixteen and my father was twenty-six, they married. They had a very fruitful life until my father died. My mother was a beautiful woman inside and out and my father was very handsome and a Talmudic Scholar. They moved to Durham, North Carolina, soon after they married, started a good business, and raised a large family. (I was the baby!)

What seems strange now—but was not then—is how they met. It was a marriage arranged by their parents, and yet they fell in love.

I was reminiscing with my siblings about my parents' life after I saw the movie, "You've Got Mail." I love this story. I laughed so hard and cried at the end, that a friend who happened to be sitting two rows behind me came up to me afterwards to tell me she was glad that I enjoyed it so much. Is there anyone out there who doesn't know that this movie describes the unfolding of an internet romance?

Arranged marriages. Love on the internet. What do you think will be the best way of finding your true love at the close of the next century?

In the meantime, I'm ordering a computer for my home. I can't wait to get on the internet. (Wink, wink....)

I Shopped Till I Dropped — May-June 1999

Like any red-blooded American woman, I have to shop. A while back, The Wall Street Journal ran an article explaining that so many people, mainly women, shop because it is entertaining, uplifting, fun. However, there are negatives. It can be very frustrating, too.

One Sunday, I decided to replace my tired and worn (i.e., comfortable) sofa and chair. That day I spent an hour wandering from sofa to sofa in the furniture store. Well, the next evening, I was back, wandering from sofa to sofa. Right away, I spotted a set that I liked, but I wanted to be very sure. So I went back a third time, and signed up. As my sales person was writing up the purchase, she told me that once furniture was delivered, it could not be returned. I staggered out, devastated. You know, things can look so different when you get them home. I spent a sleepless night worrying about what to do, but I liked the set, and had spent so much time selecting it, I knew I could not go through the process again.

As fate would have it, a few days later a friend asked me to go to another furniture store with her to offer an opinion on an item. We were standing there with the cashier when I fell in love with the most beautiful sofa set I had ever seen. I am not exaggerating. It was plump, plush, and divine. This was not a question of liking. It was real love.

I must admit I had some compunctions about canceling on the other set. But you know how it is. You do what you have to do. So now, I am very happy and will probably not need to shop for furniture again for a long time—but then, there was this adorable dining room set…..

Goodbye, Dear Store *July–August 1999*

It isn't every day you see a grown woman cry over a grocery store's closing, but I have done it twice in my life. The first time was when our family business was taken over by urban renewal many years ago in Durham, North Carolina. The second time was more recent.

You see, I shopped at the Chastain Square A&P for 15 years. Picture this. It was Mother's Day. I had some big plans that night with my niece and her family, but I was spending a quiet day at home. Looking through the paper, I saw that there was a 35% off sale at A&P. I needed a few things, so I hopped on over.

As I went down the aisles, I saw shelf after shelf empty—yes, empty. And, yes, it was a going out of business sale. I could not believe how sad I felt. But fifteen years is a long time, and I knew I would probably not see all the people who worked there again—the manager who always asked me how I was doing—Ronnie, who will be a national phenomenon as he runs in all the marathons—Chris, who always pointed out the bargains to me. Guess I wasn't the only one, because when I got up to the cashier, I said "This is so sad." She replied with great feeling, "You all will be all right."

Of course, there are all the more up-to-date, well-stocked stores, but they never lured me in. Now I have no alternative. As I left the store, I thought I heard a voice saying, "Don't cry for me Argentina—uh, Marice." And then I did start crying.

The Yom Kippur Mosquito

September–October 1999

The dining room table had been set for three the night before. I had prepared a great pre-Yom Kippur dinner. You can imagine my dismay as well as concern when both friends called and said they were homebound with raging colds.

Who was going to eat all that food? Well, as it happens, I did a good job of it—which is probably why I sailed through the fasting! But after dinner, I sat down in my living room for a few minutes and that was all it took to get bitten to pieces. It was the teeniest little mosquito you ever saw. I swatted, I swore, I batted the newspaper at him and he just would not go away. I proceeded to get ready for Temple, which was not easy because I was so busy scratching the bites. Finally, I was ready to leave when the worst of all scenarios took place. I scratched my leg, and there went my hose. One gorgeous run. There was no quick way I could change hose, so I just made up my mind to ignore the run.

I was coping pretty well until I parked my car and ran into a friend of mine. When I confided in him, he assured me that he was going to tell the rabbi to announce it from the Bema. Well, of course, he was kidding. But did anyone else see? I guess I'll never know.

The Express Lane to Trouble   *November–December 1999*

All the check-out lanes at the grocery store were long on that hot summer Sunday afternoon. But aha!—I spotted no one at the 15-item express lane. I will admit I did not count the items in my cart, but it looked like about 15, so I approached.

The cashier started scanning my purchases when a voice behind me bellowed, "Lady, you should read the sign! It says 15 items or less." I turned my head slightly to see a very tall, ferocious-looking man addressing my back. I was terribly embarrassed and thought of many retorts, but said nothing.

I am sure it added to his anger when, halfway through checking me out, the cashier had to stop and help the cashier in the next lane with the register tape. But finally she finished my order and smiled at me pleasantly. I rushed out of the store perfectly distraught, went to my car, deposited my goods, and hopped in. I started the car, looked to each side, and inched my way out of the parking space when I felt a soft c-r-u-n-c-h.

Immediately, I jumped out of my car. Lo and behold, out of three million people in Atlanta, half of whom seemed to be in this store that day, who should be standing there glaring at me, but the man who had been behind me at the checkout.

Without thinking, I put my hands on my hips and said, "Oh, it's you again!" The gentleman snarled at me and said "You know you had about eighty different things in that line back in the store." I heatedly told him that I did not. I had maybe one or two more things than I was supposed to have. So he said "Well, what are you going to do about this?" All I could see on his car was a black smudge, just one among many, but I said, "Whatever you want to do." For a minute there was silence while he carefully surveyed his car. To my complete amazement, he said, "Well, I guess it is going to be okay." I was weak with relief. Sometimes a little scratch (though I repeat, this was a smudge) can cost $5,000. I mumbled a thank-you and an apology.

The moral of this story is: Don't get into a fifteen-items-or-less lane with sixteen items, because I counted them intently when I got home and that's all I had—sixteen items!

Thoughts About Robbie   *January-February 2000*

We would be cookin' up something in the kitchen and she would imitate Julia Child, sounding more like Julia than Julia. Sometimes, she would suddenly break into a rendition of a story with a Chinese accent that none could match. She could make me laugh so hard that tears would roll down my cheeks and I'd double over.

If someone hurt my feelings or if I was feeling down, she knew just what to say. When I was up, she would rejoice with me. If I just needed to talk, she always found the time, even though she stayed extremely busy with her husband and two beautiful children. How many people can you really count on? Well, you could count on her.

Then, tragedy struck. She was not feeling good and went to the doctor, who diagnosed her with a rare form of leukemia. Her entire illness lasted just three weeks; she died on Thanksgiving afternoon.

I loved her so much! The pain of losing her is overwhelming. Last Mother's Day, she gave me a card that said "You are not my mother, you are not my aunt, you are not my friend, you are all three rolled into one."

Summertime *March-April 2000*

Everyone has something they don't like about their birthday—it's too near the Chanukah or Christmas holidays, it's the same day as a wedding anniversary, it falls on Passover and you can't really go out to eat. Well, in my case, it's in August, though near the beginning of August. It is still the beginning of the end of the summer and I hate that. I really do.

Basically, I just plain love the hot weather. No one can understand it. There was an article in the Constitution yesterday about looking forward to the cool crisp days and sitting by the fireplace. Not me—just give me the hazy lazy days of June, July, and August, and I could not be happier. I know I am in the minority, but look at it this way, you come out of a restaurant in January and you can't wait to get into your car. In the summer you stroll out into the pleasant warmth of a summer evening. How about the ol' swimming hole—what could be more invigorating? You can't compare it with the pool at the health center where the temperature inside and outside the pool is 60.

Or maybe it's because anyone close to me died in the fall of the year and I always dread seeing the leaves fall and the dreariness of the season when the weather starts to turn. Don't get me wrong. I appreciate each season. There are virtues to each one. But I do prefer summer—you betcha!

Head Over Heels *May–June 2000*

The day a friend and I went to Fernbank was an uplifting experience. We decided to stop at a department store afterwards, and gosh, was THAT uplifting for me.

After we parked, I was walking along minding my own business and suddenly tumbled over a trailer hitch protruding way out the back of an SUV. I was tossed up and around and about, and landed hard. Suddenly, I heard a very loud crack—it was my head hitting the concrete. There was plenty of blood and a crowd gathered. One of the ladies was a nurse, and she asked me how I felt. (My friend was screaming because she thought I was dead.) I calmly said I was fine, but I thought my good watch, which had somehow flown off my wrist, was broken. Everyone laughed with relief and I stood up, though a little shakily, to show I was fine. I will admit it was a scary bit of a scenario and I hope the next time I fall, it will be for Michael Douglas or some other movie idol. However, after having X-rays taken and being told that—like my watch—nothing was broken, the only thing I had to deal with was one whopper of a black eye. Actually, the colors were also red, deep pink, and purple.

I was a celebrity around the office for a few days, because no one had ever had such a glorious eye before—even the guy who took a terrible spill playing football with his son and was walking around on crutches couldn't compete with my eye. Life, like the stock market, has its ups and downs and sometimes you just have to hold on for dear life.

New York, New York   *July–August 2000*

What a wonderful town. Not a very original observation but too apt for me to care. Near the end of May, my manager took some of us to New York for the third year in a row. Of course, there was work—listening and talking to all the experts in various areas and hearing all kinds of exciting news of things on the cutting edge of unbelievable. These meetings and lunch in the executive dining room only added to the aura of the visit. We stayed in the best hotel, saw the best theater (three plays in three days) and ate at the best restaurants.

Of course, all was not wonderful—I hate to bring up something as mundane as the weather, but it was truly awful. It was cold and this was deep into May, and we were all in our Atlanta spring clothes. It was not just cold, it was raining too. I don't mean droplets, I mean a real downpour. Though we rode in stretch limos some of the time, mostly we were whistling for taxis. Do I need to tell you what it is like getting a cab in the rain in New York?

One afternoon, after turning away from the Carnegie Deli because the line to get in was three blocks long, we went to a small lunch room. After that, we headed to Broadway and were forced by the rain into a shop where they sold suitcases and other items. Now, I really needed the small suitcase I bought, but I admit that I bought it there instead of waiting until I got home because the proprietor said he would give me an umbrella with it. I really needed that umbrella to get to the theater.

When the plane landed in Atlanta it seemed to understand that it was in the South as it glided onto the runway with a hush, knowing it had left all the hubbub behind. Well, all I can tell you is New York is a nice place to visit, but…you fill in the rest.

To Read Or Not To Read? Never A Question...

September–October 2000

Have you ever curled up with a good book on a rainy Sunday afternoon? What about the long plane ride to California that zips by because you're immersed in a really great book? Or the extra hour you have to sit in the waiting room when your doctor or dentist has an emergency—doesn't the right book make you slightly less fidgety?

When I was growing up in Durham, North Carolina, there was not a lot to do except play tin can after Hebrew School, so I started escaping to the written word at an early age. I do love to read and not a day passes that I don't enjoy it, in one form or another.

Don't tell anyone but I have read every one of Danielle Steele's novels—completely mindless epistles. Please understand that this occurs late on those nights when the rest of my free time has been spent on statistical reports and in-depth study of things pertaining to the market. And I can't explain why I enjoyed so much ANOTHER CITY NOT MY OWN, Dominick Dunne's book about the O.J. Simpson trial—I think it had to do with all the celebrities Dunne weaves into the story. And I don't think I enjoyed any biography more than the one by Lee Iacocca, the famous chairman of Chrysler. The book I just finished, WHO MOVED THE CHEESE, by Spencer Johnson, MD, about dealing with change in your work and life, is absolutely worthwhile and will only take 45 minutes of your time. And, need I mention the wonderful GONE WITH THE WIND. And the greatest of all, the Bible.

It is my pleasure to act like a library. I am always happy to share a book I have enjoyed with a friend, and my sisters and I exchange books through the mail. I adore the Buckhead library, but I buy some of my books so I can take as long as I need to finish them.

And, now, I must reveal, I have a copy of the new Harry Potter book to absorb. Isn't it great that so many kids are reading now that he is on the scene?

What Are You Doing New Year's— New Year's Eve? *November–December 2000*

You might think it strange to be thinking about the end of the secular New Year when, as I write this, we are enjoying the Jewish New Year, a time of deep reflection and an awesome period of time as we ask forgiveness for our sins, intentional and unintentional. But, truly, there is a correlation here.

December 31 we are prone to make all kinds of resolutions—some quite unrealistic to their being kept—but it is a time of reflection also and aren't we fortunate to have two holidays to get ourselves "straightened out"?? Of course, one is a somber occasion and the other a whoopdedoo celebration but on both, don't you think about and honor by your prayers and your love the ones who are gone and meant so much to you? Just consider Auld Lang Syne and know that real friends are never forgotten.

It is a rare New Year's when I have not been excited about the beginning – a whole new slate on which to write beautiful meaningful acts and deeds and know that we can hope for better than the previous year. My beloved niece died last year, and her father, this year. But, now I have big decisions to make. Do I go to the big party to which a friend has invited me in Florida = or accept the invitation to be at TimesSquare at midnight on Dec. 31st – or do I finally book the cruise (and I have been on many) that I have always wanted to take over New Year's Eve—to some exotic shore – or do I stay in Atlanta and watch the market close on a hopefully higher point than it is now?

Be marshaling your thoughts – there are all kinds of polls right now rating Gore/Leiberman and Bush/Cheney – and I understand there is going to be a national survey as to what YOU think is the best way to spend this New Year's Eve?

Dishing It Out *January-February 2001*

"Tis the night before Thanksgiving and all through the house, thoughts of what I have to do float all around the kitchen. The big day brought me an invitation to my nephew's house for a 1:30 p.m. dinner. I graciously offered to bring a bottle of Clos du Bois. Oh, if only I had just left it at that.

You see, the Friday before, my department held its annual Thanksgiving feast, to which everyone brings a homemade goody. One year, I announced that I was going to bring a Jewish meat loaf. When asked what that was, I replied innocently that it was a meatloaf made by a Jewish person. Well, believe me, the annual dinner, attended by 100 people, is serious business, so this year I gave it a great deal of thought. While looking through my recipe book, I found the one my niece, Robbie, had given me a couple of years ago and decided that would be my contribution this year. I bought all the ingredients and just like magic, almost, I produced a masterpiece. I say "masterpiece" because that is the way many people at the Thanksgiving table described it—and, I hate to admit (particular as I am), it was just delicious. So back to tomorrow—Thanksgiving Day—based on the success of last week's sweet potato casserole, I boastfully told my host I would be glad to make one, in addition to bringing the bottle of wine.

Nothing went right! I don't enjoy grocery shopping, but I had to make three trips to the store because I kept forgetting things. But now, I had everything I needed. The first problem was the sweet potatoes, but I won't even go into that sore subject. The next part, mixing everything, went okay. But then I had to make the topping. Problems kept compounding, but instead of boring you with all the details, I'll just give you an example—the recipe called for 1/4 cup of butter, but instead of putting it in a separate bowl for the topping, I put it in the casserole bowl. I forged ahead though, and, practically in tears, finally put it in the oven. I was so afraid it was not going to be good that when it was done, I tasted it. Somehow or other, it was so good I ate half of it. Are grocery stores open early in the morning??

My Mama Was A Woman Ahead Of Her Time   *March-April 2001*

There is a great deal of comfort in memories. And for some reason, at the beginning of this year I thought about my mother a lot. Oh, I never forget this wonderful woman, but in the course of busy, busy days, you don't always have time for reflection. My mother took over the family business when my father died—two weeks before I was born—and raised seven children. She ran the business without any help, except for Lula, a kind of early-day nanny. My mama was both mother and father. Amazingly, she never lost her sense of humor and bright outlook on life. And she left such a wonderful legacy that my siblings and I are always quoting her.

Some years ago, I told a client something my mother used to say and was so surprised the other day when she reminded me about it. This is what I told her: "You must have money for everything—for bad times and for good times, too—for health, for fun, for sickness, for spending on stuff, but most importantly to save and invest.", Oh, and for the little blue box, too.

And there was the sampler she embroidered, which hung in our kitchen for years: "There is so much good in the best of us and so much bad in the worst of us, that it hardly behooves any of us to talk about the rest of us."I guess this is why to this day I hate gossip so much. Mama instilled in all of her children a strong sense of Jewishness. She also instilled in us a strong work ethic, which is why I guess I am, at this point in my life, still working—except I enjoy what I do so much that I can't call it work. I feel blessed to have such wonderful memories of my mama, Lena, who with her business acumen and outlook on life was a "Thoroughly Modern Millie." I am proud of my heritage—and I bet you are of yours, too.

Ah! Shangri-La! *May-June 2001*

The sky was so blue, the breeze warm and gentle, and the ship skimmed the water at a lively pace. I dozed a little and because the sun was baking me somewhat, I then jumped up and dived into the pool and had a nice swim. Then the music started and it was such a good beat I could not sit still and wandered over near the bandstand. They were having a dance contest and before I knew it, some nice gentleman with twinkling toes had taken my hand and was whirling me around the floor. Oh! I love to dance and I was just having the best time in the world when, of all things, at the end of the number, they announced that my partner and I had qualified for the finals. What a surprise! The music started again and away we went to the Latin beat of a mean rhumba. Eureka! We were pronounced #1 and our prize was two extra scoops of ice cream after dinner that night. Of course, everyone knows on a cruise you can have all the ice cream and anything else in the world to eat so I didn't think that much of this prize. I'll tell you more about that in a few minutes.

First, I want you to know that when I went back to my cabin to get dressed for dinner, there was a daily newsletter and it gave all the market statistics for that day and when I read where the market had ended, I almost fainted. The Dow closed at 15,000 and the NASDAQ at 3000. How could this have happened after the brutal performance I had left behind when I boarded the ship? My cup was running over. I was excited to say the least.

Things were getting better and better and then there was a knock at my door. I answered it and stood there in amazement as the steward brought in two dozen bright red roses. The card read "From a secret admirer." My, my, who is ever going to believe this? Especially me. Well, I took a shower, washed my hair, carefully dressed in my finest, and away I went to the captain's party. Lo and behold, when I met the captain, he asked me to join him at his table that night for dinner. Fine! And it was a delightful meal and all the people at the table were delightful. The dessert? My two scoops of ice cream that ordinarily

I wouldn't have touched since I am weight conscious, but to tell you the truth I had hardly tasted my dinner as I was on cloud nine. I was digging into that dish like there was no tomorrow and suddenly I struck gold! Well not gold—but diamond. Diamond earrings (a carat each), my prize for winning the dance contest.

Suddenly a bell was ringing, ringing, and ringing. Had we met a Titanic iceberg-- what was the problem? The ringing would not stop.

From deep under a pillow, I shot out my hand, and turned off the alarm clock. My wonderful dream was over; it was 6:30 a.m. on a Monday and I had to get up and go to the office.

Weekend Follies   *September–October 2001*

It was a painful weekend, perhaps even a lost weekend.

It's like this—I came out of my kitchen that Friday night and ran right into the leg of a dining room chair, and banged up the toe next to the little one on my right foot. It hurt—I mean, it HURT! I couldn't walk without limping, and had to take Advil so I could get to sleep. The next morning it was no better. Well, I was not going to let it keep me down, so I donned open-toed shoes and hobbled out. I went to the optical company where they had given me a sunglasses prescription that didn't work. They proceeded to tell me that nothing was wrong—they told me this over and over and over again, so I showed them. I walked out and went to another optical company, where the problem was remedied.

This all entailed lots of walking and patience, which at this point I did not have. I suffered through Sunday and finally on Monday I went to the doctor, who took an X-ray. You guessed it—the toe was broken. Do you know what you do for a broken toe? Nothing! Absolutely nothing. Do you know how many people told me that? At least a thousand—honestly. Well, there is one thing…the doctor told me to tape it to the next toe, and up to this point, it has helped. Even though I am not wearing-closed-toe shoes yet, I am getting around without much pain. I only mention all of this to try to help you if this unfortunate occurrence ever happens to you. Now, to answer all the questions about how I ran into the dining room chair in the first place—it just happened. Things do just happen sometimes.

By the way, did I mention the speeding ticket I got that weekend? The first in my whole life? Well, that's another story.

Gourmet! Oy vey! November–December 2001

It was so exclusive there wasn't even a sign out front to identify it. But we found it, and so began an incredible experience. Not one I care to repeat, but it really was something else. I was being treated for my birthday, and that was my only excuse for enjoying all the calories I consumed.

First of all, the maitre'd resembled the average successful CEO, and all the staff looked like movie stars.

Surprisingly, in such a ritzy place, the tables were quite close together, and you couldn't have a very private conversation. The people on either side of us were from out of town, vacationing in Atlanta. We were talking about the market (which I do 24/7), and the couple to my right wanted to weigh in with their thoughts, questions, and opinions.

Each course was preceded by two ounces of the appropriate wine for each dish. Ordinarily, I am a one-glass-of-wine person, but there was nothing ordinary about this night. The next day, I couldn't tell anyone what was served—not because of the wine, but because each dish was prepared in such a way that I hardly recognized anything. When the waiter brought the fourth course, I asked plaintively if I had to eat any more. He said there were only two more courses to go. Everyone around us laughed at my question, and you knew they felt the same way. Popular belief is that this place doesn't give you a lot of food. I emphatically disagree!

As I said, it was an incredible experience and I did enjoy it. But, you know what? The next day for lunch I had a McDonald's chicken sandwich and fries, and they were m-m-m good. And that night I ate lettuce and the next night I ate lettuce and the night after that—you guessed it—another salad. Oh, well, there is always a price to pay.

Bill Breman, Young at Heart January-February 2002

It was thirty years ago that I met Bill Breman. It was not a very auspicious event—I was fairly new to Atlanta and he came down to the office to see my boss, Sidney Smith—I knew nothing about him-- just treated him cordially, as I did all clients. But, what an impact he had on my life! When Sid Smith died and I became an acting broker and an associate of Harold Goldstein, Bill certainly accepted me in my new position and we all worked together very well. He and Sid were of the generation that expected and demanded excellence, if not perfection, and I sure learned to dot my i's. Harold was not of that age, but of that stage, so I stayed on my toes – I had to.

To say that I was kind of scared of Bill would be telling it like it was. After all, when I met him I was a young "thang" and a bit shy. Sid Smith probably helped me deal with Bill because I first had to learn to stand up to him – to both of them really.

Actually, we became good friends and had interesting chats on the phone from time to time—about a lot of things. Bill came up to my office one day looking very happy; he had been so sad after Sylvia died, so I was glad to see a smile on his face. He told me he was getting married to someone much younger, "but most anybody is younger than I am". He, Elinor, and I had many lunches over the years. I last saw this remarkable man about ten days before he died. I didn't think he would do that –die, that is. Does an institution die? Does someone who was so philanthropic, giving, alert, and strong actually have to die? It was hard for me then. I am writing this little story now because it will be a year in December since he's gone. I still miss him and so thoughts of him are very prevalent now.

But this story would not be complete if I didn't tell you about the time some years ago he called me up and said Marice, my account is out of balance by one cent and I want you to get that fixed right away. Yes, sir! I said and immediately walked out to my assistant's desk and told her that Bill's account was off by a penny and to check it out and find out why. She looked at me with a dazed expression on her face and said "what". I said yes and to get to it right now.

That was Bill! I will tell you I was always happy to know the answers to the questions he asked—he was always on top of things. To the end, he was mentally alert as anyone much, much younger. He was amazing. I expect to see him at certain places but he is not there. But, certainly the true great spirit of him lives on. As so exemplified by the design Elinor thought to have done in the shape of a flame from his favorite ties, which hangs in the Breman Jewish Home lobby.

Yes, he truly was a vital person – young at heart so aptly described him as played at his funeral service. I am happy to have known him!

But I Can Weather The Storm…..   *March–April 2002*

The morning of an early January day, I awakened to the tune BABY, IT'S COLD OUTSIDE – You remember it goes like this: the snow is snowing, the wind is blowing - WELL!! Sure enough, the weather report was for SNOW. I am not comfortable driving in the stuff, but ate breakfast, read the paper, and got dressed and left my house. Pretty soon after I got to the office, it started gently coming down. I was scared so I left for home pretty early in the afternoon and that was fine. The next day was a different story – We were blanketed with the white flakes. I called this friend of mine from the office and he graciously offered to come by and pick me up – he lives near me. Only trouble was when he drove up, I had to get from my front door down the walkway to his car. I was petrified – then I spotted the YOUNG guy from the condo two doors over from me and I asked him how it was walking on the snow --To prove to me that it was all right he immediately started singing and dancing all over the yard and concrete walkway and not only that, he then came up to me, extended his arm and escorted me to my friend's car ---my friend was hysterical at this guy's antics and I must say we were all in a good mood. It was fun and thenceforth, after working several hours at the office, my assistant, Cory, drove me home where I worked the rest of the afternoon.

This story would end here but the next day, thinking all the snow and ice were gone, I set out to my garage and immediately slipped as I was headed down some steps – no, this is not a bad ending – because I grabbed the railing and saved myself. HOWEVER, here comes the bad ending. The next morning (Sat.) I headed out of my garage to go meet a friend at Goldberg's for brunch and I was overly cautious and scraped my beautiful Lexus against the concrete post in my garage – Well, that had never happened before and it was pretty dog-gone upsetting. I got it fixed at the dealer and it looks fine now. Lesson 101 – You CAN be TOO cautious. And one last thought: If Winter Is Here, Can Spring Be Far Behind??!!!!!!!!!!!!

Technology-Smecknology   *May-June 2002*

It's about time for me to write about technology again. I told the girl at BellSouth DSL yesterday how frustrated I was and she said but isn't it wonderful. Sure, she works there and has to say that.

You see, it isn't only the computer – but before I leave that area, I will tell you that a component, connecting me with my office in New York needed the software put in again before it started back up (it had worked fine for two years and then stopped), and I am so happy now that I have it back. I give thanks each time it connects. You may think that's a pretty dramatic statement but- well, it's true.

- Once I got BellSouth DSL (high speed internet), I changed my email address to a BellSouth email- the day after I did that, I switched back to the AOL email I had been using before. I cannot imagine what all the people in my address book think. I don't even WANT to think. I did it for reasons I had rather not go into.

- So, now let's talk about my VCR. I got a new one a year ago and because the guy who set it up for me did it in a very complex method I have had a heck of a time, even simply playing a tape, much less recording on it. But success has arrived. After some proper instruction, I recorded Saturday Night Live last night. I actually had never watched it before—and I don't think I care to do it again, but I am thrilled I got it taped correctly.

- Now, let's talk about telephones. Gee, words fail me and that's unusual. Because of a glitch in my answering machine, I signed up for BellSouth voice mail. You put it on to ring four times before voicemail picks up—and then it rings SEVEN times. Don't ask me why!

- And how about cell phones. Great invention! If I wasn't already a cussin' woman (due to my years dealing with the market) I would have become one. I am referring to the way they cut off in the middle of a word sometimes, for whatever reason.

- And, finally, could you scream when you call a business and they give you three options—select one and then they give you five more options, select one of those and you get four more.

Excuse me, while I go out to bite my nails!

A New York State of Mind *July–August 2002*

"Give my regards to Broadway!"

As I left the office that Friday, that's what my co-workers yelled out to me. Ever since September 11, I had felt the need to go to New York. I love New York anyway and need a shot of the city every so often. But it was more than that. I wanted – no, it was a compulsion – to go and show support for everyone there. Somehow, this seemed to be the right thing to do and the right time.

Let me tell you – New York City has not lost its magic. It was alive – scintillating! Everywhere I went, the people contrary to their reputation, were so nice. I did many exciting things: saw two plays, as well as a movie I had been wanting to see, shopped at Henri Bendel, ate wonderful food. (Yikes! A breakfast of cold cereal, orange juice, and coffee cost $25. However, across the street from the Shubert Theatre, a delicious sandwich cost $4 at a really nice deli). Visited with a cousin, attended the annual shareholders meeting (the parent company of my firm, Salomon Smith Barney) held at Carnegie Hall. I asked someone how to get there and, of course, the response was, "Practice, gal, practice."

Now in Atlanta you have to be at the airport only one hour before your destination time, but in New York, you have to be there 90 minutes early. The flights both ways were right on time and smooth as glass. I felt uplifted when I left New York and was so glad I had made the trip and gotten my needed shot of the Big Apple. And, if you don't mind, I would recommend that you do the same. If not, you may always regret it.

High Holiday Memories

September–October 2002

The other night I simply could not go to sleep. Various scenes started playing across my mind. And what did these pictures concern? Growing up in Durham, North Carolina. It was such a tight-knit community, and the Jewish families were very close. My whole life revolved around the synagogue. Well, not 100%. I used to go to some YMCA dances on Saturday nights because there was a big band and big floor and plenty of guys from all the area universities with whom to dance.

But back to the sleep deprived night, I was thinking of the holidays. Growing up, we always walked to and from the synagogue. (My mother was very observant. Once, I recall that it was pouring down rain, and she told us, "We're walking.") So many acorns fell on the ground around the synagogue that, since childhood, they have symbolized the holidays to me. Also, my mother always saw to it that I had a new dress. It was a special time for us and I always looked forward to seeing all my friends at the services. Afterwards, we would come home to a wonderful meal. Of course, for Yom Kippur, I started fasting at age 13. I often say now that if someone put a scrumptious looking repast in front of me on Yom Kippur, I could not eat it, nor would I want to. It is hard for me to fast, but it is very important for me to do so.

Remembering –Just remembering. That is what I was doing that night. I felt the strongest emotion thinking of my loved ones who are gone. I miss them so much. Of course, as I am writing this, it is a very hot night in July. I haven't heard the sounds of fall approaching yet, but my thoughts were of the holidays, perhaps because they are early this year. And somehow, I felt comforted by doing just that.

Remembering. My heart was so warmed by the thoughts, and pretty soon I was fast asleep.

On Life and Lemons

Life deals blows sometimes, and it takes a lot of fortitude to survive. It helps to make lemonade out of lemons.

Like the day I left the office at 5:00 to attend an important meeting at the Swissotel. A top official from my firm was speaking to us at 5:30, and some of my clients were attending. Well, as I got in my car, one of the guys called out to me that I had a flat tire! That lemon hit me square in the face. This really nice young man said to just drive to the gas station down the street and he would follow me. Made it there – first squirt of lemon in the glass. Turns out I had a cut in the tire. No, I didn't vote for Shirley Franklin, but if she does get these pesky potholes fixed, she has my vote for life. The tire could not be fixed, and I had to replace it. Can you believe I was at my meeting at 5:30 on the dot! I squeezed the rest of that lemon in the glass and added sweetener and it tasted great.

Then there was the suitcase travail. I had one for years that I really liked but suddenly it died. So off I trot to a local emporium. The first suitcase looked nice, but when I got it home, the lemon socked me again – It was too small. I discovered this the day before I was leaving for a trip. The tag said it was 24", but it was only a 21". Rushed back to the store and bought a beautiful red one, only to discover when I got it home that there was a tear in the fabric – small, but a tear nonetheless. I used my neighbor's suitcase for the trip. When I got back, I returned the red suitcase to the store. I was able to get another red one, but after I got this one home, I discovered that one of the compartments had a broken zipper. After my third trip back to the store, the salesman couldn't stop apologizing. We picked out another and examined it from head to toe, and it seemed perfect. At last, I got my glass of lemonade.

Then I attended the first business breakfast meeting of JEWISH LIFE MAGAZINE. There was a very big crowd, and I was enjoying my breakfast and talking with people at my table. Just before the speaker began (he was really good), I decided to get a cup of coffee. When I was walking back to my table, my heel caught a ridge in the flooring. What a lemon! I went plunging forward and then plunging forward again as coffee sloshed out of my cup—miraculously, I righted myself and as I did, everyone in the immediate vicinity started applauding. So, I extended my arms in the air and took a bow. Not one drop of coffee got on my lavender suit, so I took my seat. I did have a half cup of coffee left but instead asked the waitress for a glass. Why? So I could make another glass of lemonade, of course!

Going Bananas at Work   *January-February 2003*

Hello Amigos!! We're Chiquita Banana and we have come to say--
The market needs to go up in a very big way- – We're also here to tell you, and you ought to know, the market is way, way, way too low.

What is this all about? It is about the fact that every year my company has a Halloween costume party and it is a really really big deal. The prizes are good but that is not why I have entered every single year. I just want to be appreciated for having some good ideas on costuming and content. SOOOOO. That is why I have always wanted to win first prize—never did—but felt this year I might make it.

Oh, I should mention here that not only did I not win first prize, or second or third, but came in last.

For this year's contest, I wrote a parody to the words of Chiquita Banana. I enlisted a partner – got mariaches – appropriate dress – and we practiced several times. In the midst of one practice, the manager came upon us and though he said we should win first prize because of our enthusiasm, he shushed us.

And so arrived October 31 at 9:00 a.m. and there were three judges. I shamelessly told one of the judges (had never seen him before in my life) how attractive he was. When it came to our turn, we got rousing applause during our act and I later found out that judge had given me the highest score. Alas and alack, however, we did not win a prize, not to mention first place. However, I was pretty excited because we did win fifth place.

Even more importantly, all day long different guys and gals came up to tell me how good they thought our presentation was.

Not being discouraged, I will plan to try again next year.

I just want to say two more things – If anyone wants to know the rest of the words to my take off of Chiquita Banana, they will have to talk to my recording company or buy the CD when it comes out. Also, though it is wintertime when you are reading this, would like to give you one piece of advice –

Don't, whatever you do, accept any tricks this year, go for just the treats and may 2003 treat you well.

A Simple Job Turns Monumental   March–April 2003

More than one person said to me "But, Marice, you just renovated". I patiently explained that it had been a number of years since I had done so. It sounded like criticism to me – and I can tell you I had rather have compliments. How about "How energetic of you" or how about "How nice that will eventually look" or how about "Yes, that is good and someday your property will sell for a lot more". I did not get any of those kinds of statements but I was undaunted. I knew my bathrooms needed redoing and I forged ahead.

My renovation person was highly recommended. BUT, after coming over and giving me an estimate he told me to meet him at Home Depot on a certain day, certain time, at the entrance. Unfortunately the exit looked just like the entrance and we both waited for 45 minutes in vain. Next, I decided to manage the selection of what I needed on my own and headed out to Home Depot Expo. That was a wonderful experience and I found everything I needed and wanted and all the service was excellent. After buying all this stuff, they told me to drive around to that area and someone would load my car up. I had been in the store 3 hours so perhaps you can understand I was quite tired and that is why half way home I realized I did not pick up the goods I had purchased. Yikes. Back I went and the kid who put the things in my car said three times that he thought I had forgotten to come get the packages. I said if I forgot why am I here. I am here and please don't say that again. Oh, well, I proceeded along my merry way and when I got home, I wondered how I was going to get all things inside. I found the answer – one by one I toted them into my home.

Monday a.m. at 8:00. Hank was here as we had agreed. I left for work then, happy to have things underway. From then on out, the major problem was the wall paper didn't show up when it was supposed to have been at my place. And after many calls to Home Depot Expo and Fed Ex it finally arrived 6 days later! The only other problem was having two bathrooms out of commission at one time. Not to go into detail, but this situation existed because of the delay of the wallpaper delivery. It was not easy but I won't belabor that point. You should have the picture. Things were finally completed and I expressed to Hank that I would be very happy to get it all cleaned and spiffy and neat. He could not understand as he thought he had made no mess. Ha. You should have been here.

The world of renovation is not in the category of moving – definitely not – but it is quite a world. I am so pleased with the end results that I would discourage no one from embarking on this course. HOWEVER, don't say I didn't warn you that the simplest of changes can entail a vast amount of fortitude.

A Wild Ride　　　　　　　　　　　　　May–June 2003

Many years ago, when my brother-in-law, Vic, was still alive, I went out to L.A. to visit him and my sister Helen – that was my first of several trips I have made out there. But, this one I will never forget. The reason being that Helen and Vic and Florence and Lou (friends of theirs) took me to Disney World. What a treat – walking around eating cotton candy and looking at all the sites. All of a sudden we were at the roller coaster – called Thunderbird – and Vic and Lou decided we should all go on it. Helen said she definitely would not attempt it, nor Florence – but I thought it sounded like fun.

What an experience! This thing took off – it went straight up in the air – I mean straight up – and then zoomed down and then up again and all around. I was gripping the bar across the seat next to Vic and I was screaming for all I was worth. What was I screaming? The only thing I could say was Vic, I am SCARED – and I said it over and over again. Didn't open my eyes at all – except a couple of brief times. Vic was very calm and tried to calm me down. Seemed as though it would never end. But, finally, it did. I staggered off that monster into my sister's arms. The worst part of it was that I had gripped the bar across the seat so tightly that I could not open my hands for several minutes. Never again (and never before) have I been on a roller coaster. Except it occurred to me recently that sometimes life is like that ride. Some say the market on some days in recent memory has been like a roller coaster. There are any number of comparisons I could make. Basically, though, there are days or longer, when there are tough things to deal with for all of us and it seems like there is no end to the sometimes violent ups and downs that one might encounter. It has certainly been traumatic to have a war going on and hear about armed force members being killed – then the wonderful elation of a POW being rescued or a missing in action coming home. I don't know of any remedy for all these emotions but to keep your feet solidly planted on the ground and trust in your faith to get you through., and in this case a strong belief in your country.

　　What else – a sense of humor ALWAYS helps everything.

Jesslyn, Juliette and Jake   *July-August 2003*

These are the three additions to my family in the past year or so. Juliette was born first and I have followed her progress on the internet as her mother sends me pictures. And I can never get enough.

Then, along came Jesslyn, not sisters, just cousins, and I have met her in person – twice. She has the most intent stare and the first time she looked at me long and hard – honestly, I didn't do anything, but she let out the most blood curdling scream I have ever heard. The next trip I made to her home I managed to keep her occupied for some time while she took every toy in the world out of this basket and solemnly handed each one to me. I understand==patience is a virtue. But I was well rewarded when a little later, out of the blue, she same over and planted THE biggest kiss on my lips.

Jake was just born about 6 months ago. He is very, very cute. He looks at me very seriously, too. I guess this is what babies do when they are born with so much intelligence. (Of course, I am not prejudiced).

I will meet Juliette for the first time this summer, and I am very excited about the meeting. I feel sure she will gaze at me very intently, also.

In the meantime, I have pictures on my fridge and every time I open the door I find myself smiling. I guess when I see them all this summer, I will have to take Dow Jones Katz with me. He is better known as D. J. He was a gift from a very good friend of mine and he sits on my desk trying very hard to move the market in the right direction. He is very popular throughout the office and with all my clients. Oh, he is not for real, but who cares as long as he works some magic.!!!!!!!!!!!!!!!!!!!!!!!!!!!!!

Katz, Cats, and Hats — *September–October 2003*

My mother loved to wear hats and I have fond memories and pictures of her in some nice creations.

BUT, I also remember BULL (no relation to the market) our cat when I was growing up. My mother kept her hats in individual boxes in the attic and somehow Bull found her way there – twice – to have a litter of kittens. It would have been funny but it got to be sort of untimely for the hats, and so Mom put Bull in her car and drove her out quite a number of miles to a farmhouse where she knew the people would give Bull a good home. Lo and behold, the next morning there was Bull at our front door step. Before I leave Bull, will just let you know she lived a long time and resided in comfort in her old age until the end. And, oh yes, the location of the hats changed.

A few years ago, speaking of hats again, a friend sent me some really cute notepaper, each one with a model in a picturesque hat. Because of writing a note on this paper to a friend, I just got a pin in the shape of a beautiful hat for a Chanukah gift. And that reminded me I had one hat in my closet that I had only worn once – didn't have the courage to wear it twice – but I pulled it out on the night I got this lovely little hat brooch and tried it on. Well!! I have decided to wear it again. It really does take courage, so wish me luck. You know everyone has their "thing" they love or have a weakness for – with my mother it was hats, for myself I love bathing suits. I am, however, beginning to see what tempted mom and will be visiting the hat salons more often and maybe replace my bathing suit love with hats – though I kind of doubt it.

Puttin' On The Ritz   November-December 2003

"Though we travel the world over to find the beautiful
We must carry it with us or we find it not." Ralph Waldo Emerson

People travel thousands of miles away to find happiness or whatever, and I think Mr. Emerson put it very well. When you go on a "journey" you take yourself with you. But, also, there is a point to be made for finding happiness in your own backyard – or a step or two away.

Stress can be a killer, and I needed some down time – I had had a wonderful anniversary celebration for my 40th year with my company – I had also enjoyed a "21st" birthday and lots of other summer festivities – but all of a sudden I felt the need to "get away". And I knew I wanted to have a resort "vacation" – where to go? – Well, I didn't have to think long – There had been a lot of talk around the office about Reynolds Plantation at Lake Oconee in Greensboro, Ga – and the thought had evidently stuck in my head because suddenly, I knew that is where I wanted to go. So! I made reservations at the one year old Ritz Carlton there at the Lake (and before you get the impression that I took a very expensive way to rest and relax, I must tell you my points on my MasterCard that comes with my account at Smith Barney covered my stay at the Ritz). I had two important appointments that morning and could not get away the day I left until 2:00. The drive was going well and was within ten minutes of arriving at my destination when all traffic came to an utter standstill. Ten minutes passed, twenty more, then half an hour – still at a complete standstill. I read the Wall Street Journal from cover to cover and then people started getting out of their cars, talking to each other – mainly wondering out loud when we would start moving again. Finally after one solid hour and a half, we were all on our way. I arrived at the Ritz and tired, worn out and bedraggled, I wandered up to the front desk and was greeted warmly and told that the hotel had taken the liberty to upgrade my room.

Well, needless to say that was good news and after attending the afternoon reception in the lobby for a short time went up to my room – excuse me, I meant to say BEAUTIFUL room. The whole place was a dream. I was on the Concierge level where they have a Presentation Room and food and drinks of any sort all day long.

And I could go on and on – about the wonderful staff there, about the really nice and interesting people I met, about the beautiful swimming pool, about the songstress in the lounge (Melanie Massell) and lots and lots of other pleasant experiences but – I will just say it was wonderful – and when I got back to the office, was told I looked 10 years younger and I had better not go back there or I might return wearing diapers.

Have I convinced you? Forget Europe, Asia or the Grand Canyon in Arizona – Happiness can be only a step away.

Random Thoughts   *January-February 2004*

It just blows my mind how quickly a year goes by . Was it not just yesterday that we were welcoming in 2003? And now, baby, '04 is here! At the start of 2003, I did not want to take my usual long weekend trips because of SARS and terrorism alerts. But I got over that – after all, life goes on. And so far, I have had some good trips. - Of course, the best part of going away is coming back – When you leave Atlanta, you don' go nowhere.

My gosh, I hit my 40th year with the company – I had not thought much of it – but everybody else had. There were flowers, balloons, a special luncheon at which the CEO called me up from New York and plaintively moaned that he had only been "in service" 28 years – I told him he was making great headway. Another executive called to say Frank Sinatra and I had a lot in common—WE DID IT OUR WAY.

Then, there was my birthday – all my siblings came in to help me celebrate and that was such a neat time. The first thing to greet me at the office the day of my birthday was this huge, huge, tall vase of the most beautiful flowers you have ever seen. It created quite a stir in the office – everyone wanted to know who they were from – but I could not tell them because there was no signature on the card. Very exciting, but very frustrating.

The gardenia bush in my backyard started blooming again and my Japanese maple sprouted wings. And I could sit out there and lose myself in a good book. Ah, peace!

In any event, you see there were many memorable times in 2003 – much, much more actually. BUT – the thanks I give every morning is for my good health – I am in the business of making money, but what is the #ONE most important thing in the whole world – it is your health.

Maybe this will trigger some thoughts about your 2003. But, no matter what, with all the "stuff" going on, we made it. The world may be getting crazier every day, but we have much for which to be thankful. May this New Year treat you well.

Singing and Swinging — March–April 2004

Singing has never been my forte. I do so love to sing, but I can't carry a tune. The funny thing is that I once won a talent show on a cruise. The program director was short of performers and insisted that I be a "contenda". My talent? Off-key singing.

I was a big hit because it turned out to be a comedy act—I had not planned on that, but so many things went wrong that it was funny. For example, the microphone fell apart, and the stage manager was in the wings wildly gesturing to me to put it back together—I did not know how, so he finally came out and fixed it. At one point, I forgot the words to my song; instead of being embarrassed, I burst out laughing and the entire, vast audience laughed along with me. There were other things, too, but a pleasant surprise awaited me. When I reclaimed my seat in the audience, a gentleman behind me tapped me on the shoulder. He asked if I would come to his nightclub in New Jersey and do a series of shows. After only a minute's consideration, I said no. That might have been a mistake, because soon after, a lady named Mrs. Miller became very famous. Why? She recorded an album of her Off-KEY singing and made a fortune. Sigh—those missed opportunities!

Now, dancing is a different story. I was nine years old when my older brother, Gibby, and his friend Babe Apter turned our kitchen into a dance studio one Sunday afternoon, and Babe told me I was going to learn to dance. And I did! I have never stopped dancing, even when I am home alone and the music calls out to me. Babe got married, moved to Pittsburgh, and opened a string of dance studios.

As for me, I almost ended up a professional dancer—but that's another story.

Gin Rummy! Bridge! Mahjong! Poker! Canasta!

May-June 2004

All the above are fascinating, I guess – But what I love the most is the game of Scrabble.. I find it extremely challenging – at least when playing with really good players. When I was a kid I really liked Monopoly but it was not till I came to Atlanta that I developed an addiction for Scrabble. I made friends with a couple of gals from a club at the Center and one of them taught us how to play and become experts – not bragging at all – just a truth. Every Sunday for several years – until the teacher left Atlanta – we packed a picnic lunch and went to Lake Spivey and ate good food, swam a bunch and played all afternoon – in the wintertime we alternated having supper at each other's homes and playing.

This story needs to be told because of something that happened during one game that I can never forget. As it turns out, I guess I just don't know many good Scrabble people, but my cousin is one of those. We went on a trip together (she was then living in New York) to Florida a few years ago. It was February and we were looking forward to some sunny days on the beach but it was very cold for Florida when we arrived and it was one of those times down there when it stayed quite cool -- for the rest of our stay. So, naturally we played a great deal. And one night, I challenged her on a word –we did not have a dictionary to check on the word. Isn't it funny how some things that are so trivial can lead to a major crisis. I cannot describe how angry we were with each other and all I can say it was a good thing our departure was the next day – on separate planes.

When I got back to the office on Monday I looked up the word. It is rather strange after so many heated exchanges that I honestly cannot now remember who was right and who was wrong or even the word. But the point that I make is that when we eventually talked, we were still mad at each other. BUT, we kept talking and pretty soon we were laughing too.

Final WORD – Friendships are too important—much too important-- to end over heated WORDS.

That Time, Again

July–August 2004

Summertime, and the livin' is easy. Yes, those words are from PORGY AND BESS, and they so typify the way I feel about this time of year.

You wake up in the morning and open the door to get the paper and a nice, friendly breeze wafts across your face. You go down to Bruster's for a wonderful cone of chocolate ice cream. How about dinner at a neighborhood restaurant where you can sit outside and enjoy your meal in the warm atmosphere? Or how about coming out of a restaurant at 10:00 p.m. and not having to button up your overcoat? Then, there is the swimming pool. What can be more fun than doing laps and shaping up while cooling off? Or sitting out in the backyard with a Coca-Cola and a good book? Or when it gets dark, watching the lightning bugs light up the place? A barefoot walk in the park is nice, too. And what is better than a picnic with watermelon for dessert?

With so much going on locally and in the world, you might think it is silly to believe livin' is easy at any time. But I am just convinced that things go better in summer than in any other season. I love it!

Holidays Are To Be Enjoyed — September–October 2004

As I write this, there is a CD on playing "Rock of Ages" because Chanukah will be here in a few days. I am getting in the mood. Pretty soon tho, I may be listening to Jingle Bells, as Christmas will also be here this month. I don't know what the rabbis would say but I have always enjoyed Chanukah – from a religious perspective – and it is a happy holiday – and I also enjoy Christmas because it is a happy time of year too. There are also some recent sad memories – My sister, Dot, died last year on the first night of Chanukah.

But, I wanted to mainly talk about how BUSY it gets this time of year. I will declare it seems like every party to which I get invited occurs in December. And I love all these parties – it is exciting and a real fun thing to do but as Lewis Grizzard used to say "Why don't they start the party season the first of November". There is also the fact that being Jewish I like to remember family and friends on Chanukah but of course I also like to remember my friends who celebrate Christmas – That includes some nieces and nephews who are married to non-Jewish people and their children who are being brought up in both religions. I won't even discuss if these kids are confused. Maybe it is too early to tell but they seem to be very well adjusted at this point. So, like I went to the mall yesterday – on a Saturday no less, and I drove round and round till I finally found a parking spot. However, it was a long way from Macy's front door and I suffered from wearing too high a heel.

It sounds like I am complaining, I guess, but as I started out to say, This is a happy time of year and I will just grit my teeth and go to the mall when needed. Oh sure, I know I could buy things on line but it never worked for me when I bought things from catalogs in the old days.

Anyway, frankly, I will take Valentine's Day any time. Whoops – that is really --St.Valentine's Day and what will the rabbis say about that!!!!!

A Piece of Cake? I Think Not   *January-February 2005*

Every once in a while, I go to Bruster's and get a cone of ice cream – I especially like Chocolate Chunk – It is delicious – So-0 when someone told me that the cataract surgery I was dreading was a piece of cake, I said yeah? Well I had rather have a cone of ice cream.

Considering that I have never had any operation in my whole life except on my eyes, perhaps you can understand my apprehension. I do not want to discourage anyone from having a surgery they need, but to me, that business is no piece of cake. I remember when the doctor said I needed a bunion operation and I made the decision to wear wider shoes and it did the trick, I was very happy. Mainly because I remember a friend of mine who had such an operation and a nerve was hit and boy, did she have a time overcoming that. BUT, please believe me, the number of people who told me there was nothing to it was amazing. There are so many good doctors around, one really need not worry about the outcome of most surgeries but I still say I had rather have Chocolate Chunk.

Having said all of the above, I am looking forward to some R&R at a sunny shore. Can you blame me?

The Gift of Touch

Wow-whee – what fun it was over at the Breman Jewish Home one recent Sunday afternoon. That's because Spa Sydell treated all the residents to things like manicures, facials, massages. The smiles on the faces of all the people in this group were uplifting. It was not just for the women, but the men, too.

Sydell Harris and her husband Arthur started the spa, (well, spas plural, because there are a number of them in Atlanta) some 7 years ago. The title of this article is the theme of Spa Sydell and the theme of why they were at the Home that day with many of their therapists. It was very impressive to look around and see the results that resulted. It, for sure, made not only the residents happy but others who had dropped by to help – like Lindsey Kaufman who had worked hard with Sydell to put this program into action. Sara Kogan, who is on the board at the Home, was there and pleased as she could be with all this great activity.

And, hey, you know what? Much to my surprise, the chief masseuse at the Spa, sat me down and gave me a 10 minute massage. It was a treat I had not expected, and all I can say it was sure a good treat and I can personally vouch that everybody that had a hand in this nice event deserves applause.

A Wedding   *May–June 2005*

NOT MINE – MY NEPHEW'S

It was held at the Marietta Convention Center which is where my sister, Evelyn, and her son, Arnie, and I stayed for the weekend for convenience. Hate to admit it, but I think this was my second time in Marietta!—but, then, I've lived in Atlanta for only 40+ years.

Josh is his name. He is handsome and he married a beautiful girl. First, there was a rehearsal dinner – it was dedicated to the memory of Josh's mother and Evelyn's daughter, Robbie, who died several years ago. It just seemed so unbelievable. I remember holding Josh when he was a baby and here he is about to walk down the aisle. The ceremony the next night was lovely, and the rabbi was wonderful..

And, everything would have been wonderful Except I danced every dance at the reception. I limped out of the ballroom and I promise you, it was several days before I got over such a good time. Of all the guys I had the pleasure of dancing with, Josh's wife's 84-year old grandfather was the best.

Reflecting back on it, I recalled telling the bride's father that if Everyone who got married had the same kind of foundation that Josh and his bride had and the kind of love they had for each other, the world would be a better place.

Before I sign off, let me mention I lost my shoe – like Cinderella, but mine was dancing the hora.

The Jewish Holidays — September-October 2005

Someone came up to me at Temple Erev Rosh Hashanoh, after services, and said "Well, How Are We Doing"? I answered that so far, so good, but I did not know about Yom Kippur – and the response was "yes, this is the easy part". Gosh, don't the holidays make you reflect and think and remember. And though I have been fasting since I was 13 years old, isn't it natural to kind of dread not eating for 24 or so hours. I hope no one thinks I am not a good Jew for saying that but I do enjoy eating and I have always felt I could pray better if I had a little something to eat. But, you know what, if somebody put a juicy steak in front of me about 1:00 Yom Kippur day (and I LOVE steak) I could not eat it. I am pretty observant, at least over the holidays, so as long as I can fast I will do so.

But, back to reflection, I think it is important to think how you can be a better person and strive for that goal. It is just a few days until Yom Kippur as I write this and I know that I am striving and I don't know if I will succeed. I do know the aura of this time of year surrounds me and I will hope and pray that I can achieve that goal I desire.

When I was a young teenager, I remember asking my mother about some things in the prayer book I did not understand. She suggested I go to see the rabbi – I did so. I came home from this visit and I said to my mother that I Still did not understand. And you know what-- she said to me – "Sometimes you don't have to understand – just accept". I can tell you how much that has guided me a lot in my life.

And, I will leave you with this thought – For me, the holidays are not a piece of cake, but I don't think it was meant to be easy- Do you??

The Holidays will be long gone when you read this article, but I wish everyone a Healthy and a Happy New Year.

What a Sunday! *November–December 2005*

Can you imagine accidentally tipping over a glass topped kitchen table and the glass flying off in all directions and hurtling through the air to descend into 1000 little, medium and big-sized pieces when it hits the floor? Well, it happened to me. I was so fortunate that not one piece of these shards hit me. But I stood there crying anyway – you know, the aftermath of a near tragedy.

Then, I pondered how I was ever going to get the mess all cleaned up. It took me all of about three minutes to stop crying and a-ha!, I grabbed all the necessary tools and I attacked the job with fervor and I got it done

You are probably wondering about now why I am telling you this story, especially since it occurred about a year ago. The reason is that I happened to be reading a novel and a similar incident happened to the main character in the book. Honestly. It triggered my recollection of that Sunday afternoon. It was so awful and it was one of those things that if it has never happened to you, well, you really can't identify. All I know is that I was scared and I did not just cry, I prayed too. And afterwards, I gave a prayer of thanks over and over again

By the way, I never liked that table anyway.

Pinch Hitters Help Make Holidays a Little Merrier for Christian Employees   *January-February 2006*

It was the afternoon of December 25 and I was headed for the Breman Jewish Home. Audrey Gatex, Director Volunteer Services, had invited me to come over and write an article about the Pinch Hitters. These are people who help out at hospitals and nursing homes so the staff can celebrate Christmas with their families or relax a little bit from a strenuous schedule. This group was organized by Achim/Gate City Lodge of B'nai Brith and has been in existence since 1980. When I had told people what I was going to do I was amazed at the number of Jewish and non-Jewish people who had not heard of this program. Frankly, I did not know until that day that it was sponsored by B'nai B'rith. Before I go any further I need to say that if you are interested, go to the website www.pinch-hitters.org.

The people I met were such dedicated individuals – One gentleman, Ted Spitalnick coordinates for B'nai Brith with the Jewish Home and works with Audrey. Ted has been a volunteer for 15 years! One nice lady, not Jewish, said she just loved relieving people so they could enjoy the holiday. One young guy, Josh Sosskey, was there last year and came back with his mom, who volunteers every week, because he thought it was a nice thing to do.

I asked one gentleman if he had ever had any amusing experiences doing this work and he said his wife came with him at first but the second year they asked her to vacuum and she said I don't vacuum at home so I can't do it here – her husband said he did vacuum at the Home and at their home too!

After a while, there was a rolling ice cream social and I asked a lady by the name of Mona Shapiro what she thought of this group. She immediately said that she thinks they are wonderful and there was nobody like them

It was a pleasure for me to meet these people and like Mona, I was truly impressed with them and think they are wonderful. Next year, instead of going out for Chinese food, I will go to the Jewish Home to be a Pinch Hitter and proudly so.

A Dance with Papa   *January-February 2006*

"The passing of knowledge is like a circle with no end. As elders hand down the lessons of life, they discover the innocence and exuberance of youth from their children. And, as these children become adults, they will one day be reminded that life is but a joyous dance."

The above are words written on the absolutely beautiful sculpture given to the Zaban Tower by Candy and Steve Berman in honor of Erwin Zaban. On Wednesday afternoon, November 16 this dedication took place at the Tower. With Erwin's family and friends present, Candy and Steve made the gift "In gratitude for our mentor, Erwin Zaban".

Most if not all of Atlanta know and appreciate that Judy and Erwin created an endowment in addition to the money HUD granted to rehabilitate the existing William Breman Jewish Home and to build the Tower. Some of the remarks Steve made in the presentation of this gift are so worth repeating. For example, he said, "Erwin, I have often called you the architect of the 20th Century Jewish community – Not only because of your extreme generosity, but due to your guidance and mentoring, we have been able to move the community consistently forward on a positive basis." Although Steve enumerated many of the wonderful acts and deeds of Erwin, he said that Erwin's greatest legacy was to teach and mentor those of us who aspire to walk in his steps. As to all of this, Erwin stood up and said that Steve had exaggerated his importance to the community and said that he had received much more than he had given. Does anyone doubt now why Erwin is called a modest and unassuming man?

Adam Skorecki, President of the Tower, then accepted the gift of sculpture on behalf of the Tower.

It does seem there is only one thing to say at this time – That the world is going to know about the A-T-L, a great city and they should know, too, about E-Z, a great man.

Love Led Him to Judaism   *March–April 2006*

It was not an interview the day we met. It was a journey—a lovely trip through the life of Rabbi Frederick Reeves. Rabbi Reeves joined the rabbinic staff of the Temple in July of 2005. Frederick Reeves was born into a Protestant family in Chattanooga, Tennessee, and spent his childhood there, in Columbus, Mississippi, and in Richmond, Virginia.

Frederick attended college in Williamsburg and then, thinking he wanted to pursue a career in law, went to work for a law firm in Richmond. The firm sent him on a case to Detroit, where the preparation required a Japanese translator.

A beautiful young Jewish girl named Laura applied for the job. She had lived in Japan for a while and spoke the language fluently. They started dating, and Frederick soon desired to learn more about the Jewish religion. The more he read about Judaism, the more he wanted to know. As his love for Laura grew, so did his fascination with Judaism. It is easy for us who are born Jewish, but imagine starting from scratch! However, Frederick's appetite to learn became so strong that his path to conversion and then entering the rabbinate was relatively smooth.

Rabbi Reeves believes that you make choices in life that construct your identity and certain things are beshert—such as the path that led him to Laura and to becoming a rabbi. He can't imagine doing anything else. It is easy to see that he has a passion about the rabbinate, and it is a joy to hear him expound on that subject. He loves living in Atlanta and thinks it is an energetic and progressive city, offering everything from great culture to nice places to walk. It was so appealing to hear him speak of his children—Violet, who is five and is talking up a storm; Asher, who is three and very much into pirates; and Levi, who is 18 months and just learned to say those important words: Choc-ah-chip coooookie!

Rabbi Reeves' life role is clear-cut. He feels fortunate o have been chosen to join the staff at The Temple and to be in such a wonderful Jewish community. But really we are the fortunate ones to have him in our midst.

Goodnight and Good Luck   *May-June 2006*

As a recent Wall Street Journal article said "luck is part of everything." Such as a song on a CD I have by Frank Sinatra "Luck, Be a Lady Tonight" – Such as Woody Allen's new movie in which the opening shows a tennis ball teetering on the edge of the net when the narrator says "It is all about luck". When I was at the airport on a recent trip and had to take my shoes off in the security line, I saw a dime and considered that a lucky coin. And when I was at Goldberg's deli the other Sunday and standing with a friend in a very long line, what happened? Well, the guy seating people said, "Anybody here need a table for two", and I raised my hand. Everybody else, it seems needed a table for three or more. As we walked to the front of the line, several people said, "Gosh, you sure are Lucky."

Which brings me to say, some things people call luck are just happenstance. Also, some things aren't luck, they are the result of hard, hard work. Like spending a couple of hours on a hard project that proves rewarding and someone says, "aren't you lucky"? That makes me kind of mad.

It just appears that people are so likely to label everything that turns out good as sheer luck. It certainly does play a part in our lives but it is just one aspect of many, in most cases. Personally, I feel that in life, it is so easy to say everything good that happens is due to "luck", but I say the man upstairs has the biggest direction over your life and that brings in the power of prayer.

Don't get me wrong – we can all use a healthy dollop of good luck, but let's not attribute it to everything good that happens, and by the same token when things go the wrong way, let's don't attribute it all to bad luck.

Retirement – Not Yet

July-August 2006

This summer I celebrated my 43rd year at my company. An auspicious event, wouldn't you say? Well, as things turned out, I never even thought about it till that afternoon when one of the managers called me on the phone to wish me congratulations. I asked Why? What for? And he told me it was my anniversary. Actually, I had never forgotten it before but I had been very busy that day and it came as a surprise so I said well, thanks. I had been given a This is Your Life party on the 30th year and a lovely small intimate lunch on my 40th so this was no special occasion but it really was one, wasn't it. When I left the office that day I reflected on when I first came to the company and it seemed impossible that all those years had gone by.

I must say that never once in all those years had I seriously considered retiring. I remembered the article in THE WALL STREET JORNAL about a CEO who had retired from a big company and exactly one year later, he was back at work as a CEO at another company. He commented that he had failed at retirement. For me, that might have been the same comment had I retired. It is just that I love what I do and so I never think of it as "work" but enjoyment. For different reasons, many people work past the typical retirement age these days. So, it is not that unusual any more.

At some point, one way or another, I will hang up my hat but since I started at 2 years of age, I have time to think about it.

The Circle of Life

January-February 2007

How sad it is for any of us to lose a beloved family member. My sister Dot – also known as Dottie, Dorothy, and Dahshey – died the first night of Chanukah. She had been in hospice for a week, so I should not have been jolted, but I was. It felt like someone gave me a hard kick to my stomach. So, from a big family of seven children, there are now four of us left. My family has always been close, and it is especially comforting at a time like this to still have this closeness. Visits or calls or e-mails, we manage to keep in touch!

Dot had four daughters, and they sat shiva for several days. They were devoted to their mother, and I am glad they could find some consolation from their friends.

Dot married her childhood sweetheart, Yankee, when she was 18. It was considered *the* wedding in Durham, North Carolina, at that time. The youngest in the family, I was just a little girl then, and I was overwhelmed at the beauty of the wedding. They had a wonderful life together and were very happy until the end. Yank died several years ago.

Memories mean a lot, and I am glad I have many, many of them – but nothing, I guess, eases the pain and sorrow except time.

One thing did help – we found out the day after the funeral that my brother and sister-in-law will be grandparents for the second time this summer. Life kind of works like that, doesn't it?

As the song says   *March–April 2007*

These are a few of my favorite things….

Barbra Streisand's DVD – She recorded this in 1986 at her Malibu home. Every note was perfect and every song was beautiful. I was mesmerized for one hour, and it was as if I were in the audience on the front row. She charged each person there $5,000 to attend. I was telling one of my clients about that, and I said I only paid fourteen ninety-nine – to which he replied, "1,499?" (funn-eee)

When Barbra was here in Atlanta not too long ago, I knew somebody who paid $700 to attend that concert, but she sat behind a big gentleman and could not see a thing. The money Barbra collected went to her foundation. Of course, I guess we'd all rather she not bring politics into her singing, but I didn't have to deal with that on her DVD.

Dreamgirls – What a movie! Once again, I was mesmerized. I have been a big fan of Jennifer Hudson since her "American Idol" days and am so glad she is getting proper recognition now. It isn't often that you go to the movies and people spontaneously clap again and again.

A Woman's Place – This book by Leona Blair was recommended to me, and I could not put it down. Most of this novel takes place in Israel during its struggles to become a state. Of course, there is a love interest – the main character gives up the woman he loves to go to Israel and fight for the country he loves. It was truthful and real and made me vow that I will get to Israel yet. (The book is out of print, but you can find it at the library.)

The White House – the one on Peachtree Road. Those omelets are awesome.

There are a number of other things, but space limits me. I must add, though, not to forget Bruster's chocolate chunk ice cream. Yum, Yum.

Technology – Again

May-June 2007

Yes, again and again, technology is a part of our lives. Oh, if it were only a little simpler and oh, if the dad -blamed things did not change so frequently. How can you keep up? What was new yesterday has been replaced by something even speedier and more complex today. The Wall Street Journal had a whole section devoted to this very subject one day this week. At least it was telling us that even though the cell phone was invented to talk on, now it can do so much more – watch videos, text message and a whole bunch of other stuff. Take my word – it is dazzling and baffling. And, how about Steve Jobs of Apple Computer?? He and his company have the I Phone coming out in July or August. I am actually preparing myself psychologically for this, because I may cuss about this sector of life but I want one – I got to stay in the groove, man – so I periodically say to myself or anyone who will listen – I can master that I Phone – I know I can master that I Phone, by gosh.

And master it, I will. Though I am no expert, so far I have managed to keep astride. Where would I be without my e mails from The Temple, The Jewish Federation and all my nieces and nephews. Speaking of relatives, my 5 year old niece from Richmond was visiting me a while back and one night I got very bogged down with a problem on my computer. I was trying to remain calm when Jesslyn said "Aunt Marice, I can fix that".. 5 years old!

I leave you with that thought – 5 years old.

A Desk Reveals Hidden Treasures *July–August 2007*

The other night I was looking for something in my secretary desk and I found some things that I had forgotten about.

First, there was the story I had written about my mother's life – and her death – and how much she had meant to me. I wrote this several days after her funeral. Always wanted to get it published but never did. But Marsha at the Jewish Georgian had done a splendid job of typing it up for me several years ago. That night, reading this story, memories just poured down and around and all about me.

Then, there was the thought provoking "poem" that was given to my siblings and me by our nanny – She was very earthy and did not write it but whoever did, well, I think it is great. Bear with me and see if you find it as much to your liking as I do------------

If you strike a thorn or rose, Keep a-goin'.
If it hails or if it snows, Keep a-goin'.
'Taint no use to sit and whine When the fish ain't on your line,
Bait your hook and keep on tryin'—Keep a-goin'.
When you tumble from the top, Keep a-goin'
S'pose you're out o' every dime: Gettin' broke ain't any crime;
Tell the world you're feeling fine—Keep a-goin'
When it looks like all is up, Keep a-goin'
Drain the sweetness from the cup, Keep-a-goin'
See the wild bird on the wing, Hear the bells that sweetly ring,
When you feel like sighin' sing. KEEP A'GOIN"

Maybe the nanny, Lula, gave that first of all to my mother when my mother took over the business of the store and raising 7 children after my father died.

The only other thing I want to say and I will make it brief because by now I think everyone knows how much I love summer, but that night I also found an article from the editorial page of The Atlanta

Constitution from a newspaper they published Years ago entitled "Summer's bounty too soon to end" – and the last sentence says "It Is August, A Precious Time of Last Respite".

It is now June and I know August will be here in a minute!

Spa Day at The Breman Jewish Home September-October 2007

Entering the auditorium, I was overwhelmed. There were balloons and lights on all the little trees and there were smiling faces in a roomful of people. Lots of residents were present to take advantage of everything that was offered.

And offered it was by a wonderful woman by the name of Sydelle Harris. Yes, "Miss Spa Sydelle" as I nicknamed her who has been involved in the activities at the Home for 20 years, including being on the Board at one time. She brings the services from her Spa to the residents on the last Tuesday of every month and created Spa Day three years ago.

The first person I ran into was Audrey Galex who is the Event Director at the Home and who puts her heart and soul into her job. Then I met Mr. Martin Isenberg and his wife Phyllis and I was impressed with the word she used to describe what was going on and that word was INCREDIBLE. Because no other word could have described it. I was equally impressed by Martin's contribution that day – taking pictures of everybody and he did it non stop.

Observing the pampering the residents were getting was once again impressive and one lady, Ann Lamb, told me how much she looks forward to Spa Day and that it was so wonderful and very relaxing. A lady named Billie Smith told me she is from St. Anne's Terrace but she comes to the home for therapy since "it is the best place for therapy that she has ever known". Several residents all used the same word: "relaxing."

At every nook and corner there were staff from several of the Spa Sydelles giving manicures, giving hand massages and neck and shoulder massages too. I asked several of the staff what made them give up a day of rest on a Sunday to do this work and they all said the same thing – wanting to give back to the community and wanting to make the people at the Home feel good... Kimberly Hard, the director of the Park Place at Perimeter Spa Sydelle put in a lot of time arranging the musician, food and staff who would attend., The musician was Doug Jervy and he played and sang throughout the event and did a great job. Kimberly and I even joined him in singing New York, New York which was not too good because she and I can't carry a tune.

Oh, me, oh my, what a wonderful, joyful day!!!!!!!!!!!!!!!!!!!!

Moving!!!!!!!!!!!!!!!!!!   *November–December 2007*

Twenty-five years ago, when my office moved from the First National Bank Building downtown to the Atlanta Financial Center in Buckhead, I cried. We came in on a Sunday to unpack, and at that time I couldn't see all the advantages of and conveniences of being in our new area. I just knew I was going to miss the excitement of being on Peachtree Street.

Fast forward to October 2007. This time we moved just a block and 1/2 south of where we had been to the new Terminus Bldg. on the corner of Peachtree and Piedmont. Everyone had been asking me if I were sad to be leaving our "old" home and I said no, no – I like "new". Well, it did not quite work out like that – at least at first. Oh, sure, it was all state of the art – Walk into your office, and the lights come on automatically – walk out and the lights go off. I just missed how comfortable I had been in our old office and as my six year old niece, Jesslyn, said to her grandmother the other day, "Sometimes I get frustrated" – that is the way I felt – frustrated. I came in the first business day and I stood in the middle of the reception room – pondering if I should go to the right or left. One of my colleagues passed by me and burst out laughing – he is a really nice guy but I stomped my foot and said "Don't laugh at me" – well, he laughed even harder.

It has been three weeks now and I am happy to say I am now acclimated. Not that I get to look out my window very often because I am so busy, but the view from being on the 19th floor is absolutely breathtaking ! and I appreciate how much the lights going off automatically helps the environment.

As I always tell my clients, the one thing in life you can depend on is Change. Progress is not always easy and not always for the good, but now I love my new surroundings and maybe it was easier for the ones in my office who are in their 20s, but maybe not.

Nieces and Nephews and Nieces and Nephews

January-February 2008

There are a lot of nieces and nephews in my family and they are bright and good looking and wonderful and of course, I am prejudiced in this regard. Then, there are several who are married and have adorable little ones or babies and I get the biggest kick out of them. Especially the things they say and do. Of course, everyone feels that way about their kids and I find them appealing, too. One of my great nieces, who lives in Atlanta, is just 7 1/2 months old and her father and mother have been bringing her over periodically since she was born. Last time she was at my place she managed to get a pierced earring off my ear and ate my finger and was good as gold while we ate brunch.

Ran into this couple I know at the airport on a recent trip I took, and they were telling me about having their 9 yr old grandson and his 6 year old sister spending the night. Because of something the littlest one said during the evening, my friend told her grandson that the little girl was tough – he said to her, "Yeah, but suppose you had to live with her all the time".

Perhaps it is because they learn the computer at age 3 or have real smart mommies and daddies, but it amazes me how much kids know these days. Like one of my colleagues has a 6 month old daughter who pulls on the edge of her nanny's apron to let her know when she is hungry.

And, just think, one of the cute babies in this country will be President of the country one day – or at least the American Idol. Blows my mind.

Do the Seasons Really Matter?   *March–April 2008*

You know that old saying?---If winter is here, can spring be far behind? Well, it is January now so I keep thinking of March and the new season and I long for it. I am not trying to rush the time away – the cold days are invigorating but just not my favorite time of year. Even if we do have to deal with income tax – at the least the payment in April.

And there is Passover in April – a holiday I really appreciate – and this year especially so since I will be spending it with a niece and her adorable little ones. But this holiday appeals to me most because it is about Freedom –free from tyranny in the old days, but also represents the ability to free oneself from ties that bind or whatever your heart desires and the courage to do things that can make you a happier person. This is kind of a silly thing to want to do in the context I am discussing but you know what I want to do? I want to learn to tap dance. Several years ago, a young girl-a temp- came to my office for a short period of time—but she could really tap dance and she taught me some steps. For some reason, that is a hidden desire of mine, so don't tell anyone.

And this spring, I will be finished with some ole dental work that has lasted awhile and hopefully will have lost the elusive pounds I want to shed by then. There is a song from quite a number of years ago called "It Might as Well be Spring" -. Referring to feeling so good. And I like to think, and I find it comforting to do so, that if you have wonderful Spring in your heart, well whatever the season – it jus' don' matter.

What's New!?   *May-June 2008*

Coach is a very fine producer of leather goods. I had been using my briefcase, made by them, for about 20 years, when some of my youthful colleagues started making fun of it. I will admit it had lost its luster and had a small hole in one corner BUT it had an awful lot of character. Finally, though, I DID IT. I went into a store and bought a new brief case. Well, that was some years ago and it is nice enough, but I will never feel the same about it as my old one.

My camera was next. Quite often I would take pictures in the office and none of these kids could believe I was still using an "old-fashioned camera" (which incidentally I loved). Here again, my camera took this abuse for some time, and finally I went to Wolf Camera and looked at a digital camera. I will tell you it looked pretty complicated to me. So, I left the store and came back the next weekend and studied on it some more. Can you believe, it was only after the third visit that I half heartedly bought the danged digital camera. It came with a printer free of charge and I happened to hit a special one day only sale price on the camera. I am just beginning to get used to this high-tech picture-taker and I think longingly of my old camera.

Then, there were all the comments about my elderly adding machine. I loved it because it had adding machine paper and you could actually review and check your figures. My partner at the office would not let up on me for using such an ancient machine. I still miss it.

And then came my Rolodex. You should have heard them about it. I have persevered, however, and I have still happily and efficiently used my Rolodex. Of course, I hate to admit, but it may not be around very much longer either. I KNOW all these fancy new technological gadgets are here to stay. Hooray?

The Rush of Time — July–August 2008

How do you explain the above? The thing is it just happens I think as one gets older, but that is not exactly true because kids think the summer off from school whizzes by. All I know is that birthdays are coming much faster than they used to. And just like the kids treating each summer day as precious so too do the days get more precious when you are an adult and going through the second or third act of your life..

It even says in the prayer book "Life is but a fleeting moment". So I think it makes a difference as to how we make choices, as for any time in life really. People are always saying to me "Why don't you just travel all the time?" It gets tiring because I am asked this question so often and as I tell them I am not a traveler and never have been. I have always favored long weekend trips – not always – but mostly. If what you do, thru volunteer work, kindness to those less fortunate or actual employment, helps people, I personally think this is a good choice. All I know is I feel good about what I do and hope you do too. And if you have learned and profited from your mistakes in the past, or are still trying to accomplish that, what could be more meaningful?

People seem to like my articles more when they are funny, but once in awhile I get philosophical. Have a good summer.

The Holidays this Year....   *September–October 2008*

....were different for me from all my other holidays

It was like this—I had invited a friend over for dinner Rosh Hashanoh Eve and we planned to go to early services. Two weeks prior to the holiday, I came down with a lulu of a cold. Best laid plans, right? So I had that cold for a tad over two weeks and didn't even make dinner as I had planned, much less go to Rosh Hashanoh services. I had to stay home from the office during this cold and still didn't get much rest because my air/heating unit had broken down and the technician was there to fix it four days in a row. I was very happy I was feeling better and could eat a good dinner Erev Yom Kippur but the next morning I did something I have never done before. I have been fasting since I was 13 years old, so I hope you can understand how hard it was for me.....

.....To have a bit of breakfast Yom Kippur morning. I had to take some medicine and felt it was wise for me to do so. I prayed extra hard so some good came from taking care of myself. Yom Kippur is an awesome holiday and I was uncomfortable even with the small amount I ate but I knew it was for the best.

As I said, the best laid plans oft times gang astray. We all have to roll with the punches once in a while.-- That suggests another story. I will tell you that story another time.

Happy Days are Here Again   *November–December 2008*

First, there was my anniversary at my company. Then, there was a milestone birthday, with visits from family and Rabbi Berg at The Temple saying a blessing over me. So many people were doing really kind things that my cup did runneth over.

Best of all, I got a new nephew! I went to see him when he was just two or three days old, and do you know what he did? He actually took my finger in his little bitty hand and held it. I was amazed, and he got hold of my heart right then and there.

Then, it got to be September, and I was still swimming outside because the weather was so nice. And I could look forward to the High Holidays and the New Year.

And now, I offer best wishes to all for a healthy, happy, and prosperous New Year and a Happy Chanukah.

Maybe, just maybe, to cap all this good stuff, I will win the lottery, or the market will start looking better and have more up days than down ones. Or, maybe, I'll just say thank you to G_d, because I'm such a lucky girl.

Reminiscences　　　　　　　　　　　　*January-February 2009*

As I write this, it is just a couple of days before the New Year is here. What a weird '08. My gosh, who could have imagined it. Of course, there was the financial crisis or I guess I should spell it crises. Pillars of strength were decimated. The evil of Bernard Madoff was brought to light – so many wonderful people, charities, institutions were hurt very, very badly. So many people lost jobs and so many, their homes. A new old war in Israel? Will peace never come to this tiny country?

And, yet, I see a silver lining. I have hope and I have faith that 2009 will be a better year. It won't be perfect. Everything won't get better immediately. However, having lived through a number of bad times, I honestly believe that we will eventually overcome. January 20th will see the inauguration of Barack Obama and no matter your political persuasion, surely a new broom sweeps clean, and you have to be thrilled by this historical event.

The whole world has been injured and everyone wants a fix and I pray that will happen soon.

I once had a client say something to me years ago that I have never forgotten. Now, keep in mind, she did say this tongue in cheek and with a smile in her voice but she said to me "Marice, if you don't stop being such a Pollyanna, I am going to slap you in your face. Well, she is dead now but if she were alive, I guess I would be getting slapped in the face.

On A Clear Day... *March–April 2009*

You can see forever. And it was so at my cousin Gail's wedding. It was in Waverny, Connecticut at a century old mansion, It was a perfect Fall day and the wedding was held outside under a beautiful blue sky, not a cloud in sight. There was a rolling green lawn as far as your eyes could take in.. The bride was lovely and the groom, handsome. A nice touch to the ceremony was the rabbi singing a love song, accompanying himself on the guitar.

The reception afterwards was a lot of fun and I was especially intrigued by a gentleman I met who was a good friend of the groom. This friend was a magician. He asked me to think of a card number and I picked the Ace of Spades. After shuffling through two decks of cards, in only minutes what did he come up with but the Ace of Spades. I had not whispered it to anyone or even kept it in my mind as I was busy watching him looking through the cards. I had never met a magician before and I was truly overwhelmed by his cunning.

After a delicious dinner, I danced all night – with all the men and my 5 and 6 year old cousins.

And guess who caught the bouquet.

A Pleasant Encounter   *May-June 2009*

On my return late January from a 7 day cruise (yes, I finally succumbed to a longer vacation than usual) (and yes, it was wonderful) I was sitting in the Ft. Lauderdale Airport waiting for my zone to be called so I could board. I was ZONE 9 – When I finally heard the attendant announcing my zone, I proceeded forward. At the same time a Catholic priest walked up and said to me that it looked like we were the last two. Which was true, and I laughed.

When I found my seat, I started thinking that it would be interesting to talk with this gentleman and how nice it would be if he sat in the empty seat next to mine. Unbelievably, that is exactly what happened. We started talking and he had a terrific sense of humor. I asked him what lead him into going into the priesthood and he told me he could not get a date. He next asked me my favorite type of vacation and I told him swimming in the ocean and relaxing on a beach. He said Well, have you ever been to Israel. I admitted I had not. He told me what a wonderful experience it would be for me and that there was a wonderful beach in Tel Aviv and it was not far from Jerusalem where I would meet people at the Synagogue. That sounded very appealing since I am not big on Just sightseeing.

He then began needle pointing. Yes, indeed. A beautiful piece of work which was for his brother's birthday. Of course, I know macho men aplenty needlepoint but I had never met one. We got into discussions about a number of other things and next thing I knew we were landing. I was sorry my nice experience with a new friend was coming to an end. But, actually, I did talk with him once since then and he told me he accidentally left the needle point on the plane and nobody turned it in.

What a shame.

SO! Don't you think it was amazing that it took a Catholic priest to inspire me to go to Israel.

A New Baby In Town   July–August 2009

On a Sunday in the middle of May, I set out to see my business partner's new baby. Gage had been born a few days before. I did not know it was raining till I pulled out of my garage. Oh, well, I thought, what is a little rain. However, the more I drove, the less I could see because it was one of those pelting rainstorms that does make it hard to see. I kept thinking and wondering if this trip was really necessary. I will answer that in a minute. I kept at it and was very proud when I got to the right street in Roswell and the right subdivision. I parked my car and ran up to the front door and rang the doorbell. No one appeared at the door; I realized I was at # 1l01 and needed to be at the house on the other side of where I was standing in the pouring down rain. I slushed my way over and only a barking dog answered my ring.

Do you feel all wet by now? I Was SO drenched. I then called the proud papa and told him I needed directions. Turns out that I should have been at 110 and not 1101. A simple mistake but I am wet and still wondering if it was all really worth it.

Now, to answer that question: The minute I walked into the right house and was given a towel to dry off I immediately fell in love. This little baby boy was beautiful. Cory had described him as such but I thought he was just being naturally exuberant. But the little baby was beautiful and I immediately knew my trip had been worthwhile. I held Gage for about an hour. I did not move and neither did he, and I was in heaven. Just one more thing, every time Mozart, Cory and Leslie's little dog, put his paw on my knee I fell in love with him too. I might not get a baby but this little dog was very very cute and maybe.....

It Was Fun! *September–October 2009*

Quite a number of years ago, one of the girls in the office was retiring, and the manager invited several of us to a luncheon to celebrate the occasion. She was talking about what she was going to do next, and several attendees joined in, speculating about what they would do when they took that step.

None of this chatter impressed me. When people would ask me what I planned, I told them that I loved my business, and I was never going to retire. And I meant that.

Even years later, when I needed a partner to help with my expanding network, it took a long time to find the right person. I wanted someone to carry on my legacy, someone with whom my clients could feel comfortable, if I ever took the unlikely step of retiring. I told the manager that I guessed I would just have to stay on the job forever if I couldn't find this individual. He thought that was a good idea, but did not think it would work. Well, eventually, I found the right person. I occasionally thought about hanging it up, but not too seriously.

So-oo-ooo, it came as a surprise to me that, lo and behold, after 46 years with the same company (though with a number of name changes), some projects that deeply interested me appeared at the same time I had an overwhelming desire to call it a day and pursue other avenues.

To bring this tale to a happy ending, I will observe one more Labor Day and retire on October 1. It will be a major transition, but I tell people in the office that when I turn over for another snooze on a cold January day with three feet of snow on the ground (hmmm.....OK, maybe 2 feet) I will cry for them plowing through it all.

New Beginnings　　　　　　　　　*November–December 2009*

The Jewish Holidays have come and gone and hopefully we are all inscribed for a good and healthy year. Now, December 31 is, shall I say, around the corner…when lots of people make New Year's resolutions and drink lots of wine.

All this by way of saying it seems a good time for new beginnings. And I have started just that since I retired on October 1. I have been very busy. That is good because I don't have too much time to think of all the people I am missing. People I saw every day. I am happy with retirement. I loved my business and I worked for many, many years. Now I feel a certain amount of freedom and am at peace with this major change in my life.

In my last article, I mentioned I would be cozy and warm under my comforter and awakening at late morning hours. However, guess what? You don't need to be jealous any more. My internal alarm clock is still going off at 6:30 a.m.